Village Walks

in

CAMBRIDGESHIRE

Village Walks in
CAMBRIDGESHIRE

Jean and Geoff Pratt

COUNTRYSIDE BOOKS
NEWBURY, BERKSHIRE

First published 1997
© Jean and Geoff Pratt 1997

COUNTRYSIDE BOOKS
3 Catherine Road
Newbury, Berkshire

ISBN 1 85306 455 6

Designed by Graham Whiteman
Photographs and maps by the authors

Produced through MRM Associates Ltd., Reading
Printed by J. W. Arrowsmith Ltd., Bristol

Contents

INTRODUCTION   8

WALK

1 UFFORD (5½ or 3½ miles)   10

2 SUTTON (4 miles)   14

3 GREAT STAUGHTON (5½ or 1½ miles)   18

4 EASTON (3½ miles)   23

5 ALCONBURY WESTON (3½ miles)   27

6 BUCKDEN (4½ miles)   31

7 ABBOTSLEY (5 or 4 miles)   35

8 GUILDEN MORDEN (4 or 2½ miles)   39

9 WISTOW (5½ miles)   43

10 ELSWORTH (6 miles)   47

11 BENWICK (3½ miles)   51

12 HOLYWELL (5 miles)   55

13 BARRINGTON (5½ or 4 miles)   59

14 UPWELL (2 miles)   64

WALK

15 LITTLE THETFORD (4½ or 2½ miles) 68

16 LODE (4½ miles) 72

17 BALSHAM (4½ miles) 76

18 PRICKWILLOW (5½ miles) 80

19 BURROUGH GREEN (4½ miles) 84

20 SNAILWELL (5 miles) 88

✿✿✿

Publisher's Note

We hope that you obtain considerable enjoyment from this book; great care has been taken in its preparation. Although at the time of publication all routes followed public rights of way or permitted paths, diversion orders can be made and permissions withdrawn.

We cannot of course be held responsible for such diversion orders and any inaccuracies in the text which result from these or any other changes to the routes nor any damage which might result from walkers trespassing on private property. We are anxious though that all details covering the walks are kept up to date and would therefore welcome information from readers which would be relevant to future editions.

AREA MAP SHOWING THE LOCATION OF THE WALKS.

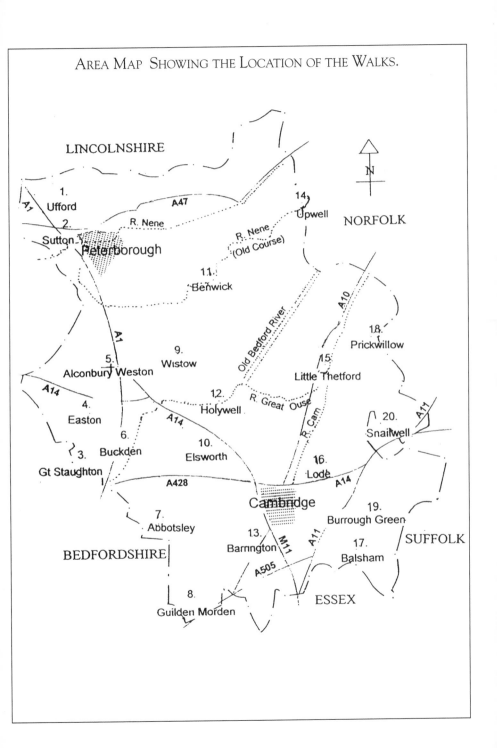

Introduction

Cambridgeshire villages vary widely in their sizes, histories and the patterns of their development. Much depends upon the topography and geology of an area. Amid the chalk hills in the south of Cambridgeshire you can see examples of the use of flint as a building material, while villages in the north-west tend to be built of Barnack limestone which gives them an attractive patina of age. By contrast, the villages of the fens have been founded and settled in more recent times – there are few, if any, old dwellings and the location of the villages and their pattern of settlement has depended on the rivers and drainage of the area.

These 20 walks, spread across Cambridgeshire, will take you to a range of attractive villages, each with different points of interest. Some have old and historic dwellings, some have broad and attractive village greens and some have interesting river frontages. Some villages are probably little known except to their local residents. You will see wild flowers, trees and maybe birds and wild animals that you are unlikely to see by the roadside or even in rural honeypots in the country.

Roads are no fun to walk on, but the public rights-of-way network will take you far from the noise and fumes of petrol and diesel engines, deep into the countryside. All the walks are along public rights of way or permissive paths which are usually well used and waymarked. However, in some parts of the county, there are places where the waymarked paths do not follow strictly the rights of way shown on the official map. In such cases, the walks are described as following the waymarked paths, which are the paths used by local people.

Please respect the countryside and follow the Country Code, shut all gates and keep dogs on leads.

Conditions of footpaths and bridleways can vary depending on the season, the weather and the amount of usage. All paths can be wet, muddy and puddly at times, and in summer can become narrow and obscured by growing vegetation. Moreover, although they should be kept clear, some field paths can become obstructed by crops. Stout footwear is a good precaution.

Reference to a stile, bridge or other detail in a walk description is intended to help clarify the route. However, where the way is clear to see, such details are not always mentioned. Similarly with the sketch maps, which are not to scale, not all hedges, fences, etc. are depicted.

Each pub and restaurant mentioned in the Food and Drink section has been visited and can be recommended. Apart from the National Trust restaurant which has special opening days, the pubs and restaurants mentioned are usually open at lunchtimes for meals, and the pubs are also open in the evenings. A few pubs have a day, or maybe an evening when they don't serve meals, so it is as well to check by phoning.

Where pubs are serving meals dogs are excluded. When dogs are permitted in a pub it is appreciated if they are kept on a lead.

Few villages are equipped with public car parks. We have indicated where we think cars could usually be left safely.

However, readers should be careful not to cause obstruction to residents or other road users. Remember that today's agricultural machinery moving along rural roads can be of enormous size. Pubs and cafés have customers' parking space. If you intend to leave a car at a pub car park whilst out walking, it is advisable to consult the landlord first.

For each walk the number of the relevant Ordnance Survey 1:50 000 map is given. It is intended that this be used, together with the sketch map in the book.

We acknowledge with thanks the help given by members of the Cambridgeshire County Council staff in the Rural Group, who look after the rights of way in the county.

In conclusion, the authors hope that this book will help readers to explore the interesting county of Cambridgeshire and that they will have many enjoyable walks.

Jean and Geoff Pratt

UFFORD

Length: 5½ (or 3½) miles

Getting there: Ufford is 6 miles north-west of Peterborough. Using the A47 Leicester to Peterborough road, 1 mile east of the A1/A47 interchange take the minor road for 3 miles through Southorpe, and just beyond it, turn right for Ufford.

Parking: There is a little parking at a bend by the church, and round the bend beyond Newton Farm on Marholm Road. Ye Olde White Hart has a large customers' car park.

Map: OS Landranger – Peterborough 142 (GR 094040).

Ufford is an attractive village set on the slope of a hill in a somewhat wooded landscape, where the land falls away to the river Welland, 2 miles away. At the top of the hill, dominating the scene, is St Andrew's church, and on its eastern side is the large former rectory. Part of your walk will be along the Torpel Way, named after Roger de Torpel who held the living of the church in the 12th century. Near the bend by the church are several substantial stone barns, converted to dwellings, with ornamental pierced stonework. They belonged to Newport Farm and were built around

1770. Then near the bottom of the hill, on the eastern side of the road and set back about 50 yards are two sides of what was once quite a large dovecot. You can see the many shelves or pigeon holes where the pigeons roosted. At the foot of the hill, on the Walcot Road, is a stone archway and opposite, at the edge of Ufford Park and dating from 1540, is a rain shelter for churchgoers walking from Ufford Hall across the park to the church. On the side of the barn opposite the inn is a quaint legend: 'The gift of Mrs Ruth Edges, to six decayed gentlewomen for ever 1724'.

This walk is along well-marked farm tracks and headland paths, going first to the attractive hamlet of Ashton, and then, skirting Bainton, to Barnack, a village built almost entirely of the local stone to which Barnack has given its name. Halfway round, and missing out Barnack, a short cut leads back to Ufford, making a walk of 3½ miles if you wish.

THE WALK

❶ Start at the bend in the road near the church. Go to the eastern side of the road, climb the bank and walk down beside the houses, passing picturesque Rectory Cottage, the Parish Hall and later Ye Olde White Hart on the right. Keep on the road through the village and near the bottom of the hill pass Ufford Hall with its converted stable block on the left.

❷ Just after Honeysuckle Cottage on the right, go right on a hard farm track which soon swings left to cattle pens. Here keep straight on, along a wide grassy headland track, with a hedge on the left. Keep on the track which, in about ¼ mile, swings left through a wide gap in a hedge and then continues with the hedge on the right. At a cross-hedge go over a stile, beside a gate. Very soon there is a wood, The Jubilee, on the right.

❸ Leave the field over a stile and turn left to walk for ½ mile along the wide verge of the road, to Ashton. Go left at the three-way road junction in Ashton.

❹ In 200 yards, where the road bends right, keep straight on. Look out for a sign and cross a stile following the Torpel Way, across a pasture. Go through the gap in a line of trees to the far side of the field. After crossing a stile follow the hedge on the right on a headland path for about 50 yards, then continue on a cross-field path, for about 300 yards to a stile which leads to a road.

Cross straight over the road to another stile and a wooden footbridge to continue on a grassy headland with a hedge on the left. At the corner of the field go through a gap in an intermittent hedge to a junction of paths.

❺ At this point, for the 3½ mile shorter

Rain shelter at Ufford Hall.

option, go half left on a reinstated grassy cross-field path. At the field boundary go slightly left and follow the headland with a hedge on the left. At the road turn right and follow the road round to the left back to Ufford.

Continuing the main walk, turn right on a headland path with a hedge on the right. At the next field corner go left following a hedge on the right, and at a waymark go straight on along a narrow footpath and enter The Synhams, a small wood. Leave the wood at a timber bridge and turn right, along a headland with a fence on the right. In under 100 yards, swing left and continue on a headland path, now with a hedge on the right. At a corner, turn right onto a farm track and walk out to the road.

❻ Turn left towards Barnack. Walk along the road for about ¼ mile, and at the junction with Main Street, turn left and walk into Barnack village. Follow the road, and opposite the churchyard, near a telephone box, go left on a narrow footpath beside the post office. At first, the path has walls on both sides but later becomes a very pleasant leafy lane which ends in the corner of a large field.

❼ At this point go left on a well-used headland path. with a hedge on the left. At the field corner go right and in about 10 yards bear round to the left, onto another headland path, still following a hedge on the left. Go right at the next field boundary on a broad headland, which soon widens to become a cart track.

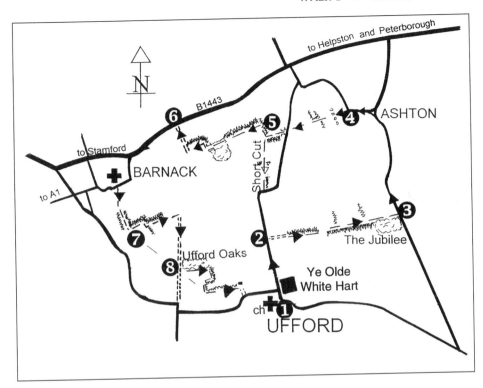

❽ In ¼ mile pass a wood, Ufford Oaks, on the left and at its end, turn left over a wooden bridge and take a headland path beside the wood. When the wood ends, turn right and keeping a hedge on the left, follow the headland round several corners of this large field and eventually you will be following a line of electricity poles. Go over a stile and keep on beside a hedge on the left. Cross another stile, passing a house, and then swinging round on a gravel drive out to the road and turn left. Walk into the village back to the start.

PLACES of INTEREST

Barnack Hills and Holes is a large National Nature Reserve, on lime-rich soil, on the edge of Barnack. It extends over 50 undulating acres, managed by English Nature, and is where the famous Barnack stone was once quarried.

SUTTON

Length: 4 miles

MANOR ROAD

Getting there: Turn southbound off the A47 Peterborough to Leicester road, about a mile east of the A1/A47 interchange. In a further mile turn right at the first turning and in a quarter mile go right to Sutton church.

Parking: There is a small amount of parking at the end of Nene Way by the stone churchyard wall.

Map: OS Landranger – Peterborough 142 (GR 095987).

Sutton is a small isolated village on the north bank of the river Nene. Although close to the main road it is an oasis of peace; only those intent on seeing Sutton would turn into the village, as the roads lead nowhere else.

At very many places in this well cared for village you will see houses and garden walls made of the beautiful grey/golden stone which used to be quarried at nearby Barnack, a village about 4 miles north. Some of the walls are dry stone walls.

A somewhat unusual feature of St Michael and All Angels' church, half-hidden at the end of Nene Way behind tall lime trees and a stone wall, is the bell-cot, containing not only the bell but the wheel which is instrumental in ringing it. On the right of The Drift is a small stone-walled enclosure; a plaque on the gate marks the old village pound which was 'Originally used to impound stray animals.

These could be claimed by the owner on payment of a fine.'

The Nene Way is an 86 mile path from Daventry to Whittlesey along the Nene Valley. This walk follows part of the Nene Way, passing close to Wansford station of the Nene Valley Railway where there is an exhibition. The path then follows the railway line and later the bank of the river to Water Newton where, close to the church and the picturesque mill, is a lock. The return is along country lanes, part of which follows the route of Ermine Street, a Roman road which ran from London to York.

THE WALK

❶ From Sutton church, turn down leafy Lovers Lane at the east end of the churchyard. Pass the village Reading Room on

The river Nene.

the right and, on the left, a secluded grave-yard.

❷ At the end of the lane go right over a stile following the Nene Valley Path. Go through a pasture beside a wood on the right. At the end of the wood, reach a line of trees across the field and turn left towards a stile in a fence. Continue roughly in the same direction to a wooden footbridge. Ahead is a viaduct where the Nene Valley Railway crosses the river Nene. Under the viaduct use a boardwalk which leads to the foot of a flight of steps on the far side.

❸ Turn right up the steps to rail level and cross the river to reach Wansford Station, the Railway Exhibition area and other facilities. Having explored the station, retrace your steps across the bridge and down the steps. Use the boardwalk straight ahead beside the viaduct. Climb the embankment on rough timber steps and at the top, walk beside the railway for almost ½ mile.

❹ Cross a stile, still keeping beside the railway. Under the grid lines cross another stile and turn right on a headland path with a fence on the right. Turn left at a

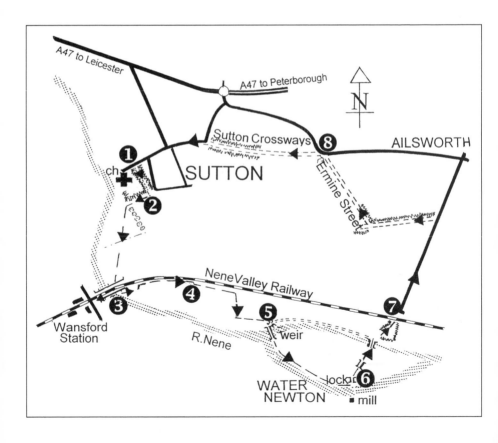

PLACES of INTEREST

Sacrewell Farm and Country Centre, just east of the A1/A47 intersection, has a working water mill, a rural museum, nature trails, and of course lots of animals. It is open throughout the year (Telephone: 01780 782254).

   The Nene Valley Railway Museum and café at Wansford is usually open on railway operating days. Thomas the Tank Engine can sometimes be seen. Telephone: 01780 784444 or pick up a leaflet/timetable at a Tourist Information Centre.

   About 6 miles away, beside the river Nene at the edge of Peterborough, is **Ferry Meadows Country Park**. A 500 acre area of lakes, meadows and woodland where a wide range of land and water-based activities is available. Entrance and car park is at Grid Ref 150972.

---

corner to continue along the headland for about 200 yards to cross a stile into a field beside the river Nene.

❺ Within a few yards swing right on a grassy path to cross a wide concrete cart bridge and then keep beside the river on the left. Shortly go left on a long timber footbridge over a weir and continue with the main river on the right. Pass a willow plantation and soon you are on a grassy river bank approaching Water Newton

Lock. Note the fine views of the church and the mill, now converted to dwellings, on the opposite bank.

❻ Go left at the downstream lock gate, and cross a wooden footbridge followed by a concrete one, and keep beside a hedge on the left, to cross a wide cart bridge over a branch of the river Nene. Turn right and then follow a hedge on the left through a tapering pasture. Go through a green steel gate and cross the Nene Valley Railway.

❼ Keep straight on along a lightly trafficked road with wide verges. In just under ½ mile, at a sign which reads 'Circular Walk', turn left along a gravel farm track. At a T-junction of tracks turn right along the route of the Roman Ermine Street, the forerunner of the Great North Road.

❽ The path comes out to a road at a right angle bend. Do not join the road but turn left along Sutton Crossways, a cart track with a hedge on the left at first. The track ends at a bend in a road. Here bear left and continue straight along the road back to the church and the start.

GREAT STAUGHTON

Length: 5½ miles (or 1½ miles)

Getting there: Great Staughton is north-west of St Neots. Leave the A1, which bypasses St Neots, at the B645 junction. Keep on the B645 for just over 3 miles.	Parking: The village car park is at the bend in the B645 road at the far edge of the village. There is plenty of customer car parking behind the White Hart pub.	Map: OS Landranger – Bedford etc. 153 (GR 113645).

In the centre of this interesting village is a lofty stone pillar, which from a casual glance might be a memorial or perhaps a mile post. It is, in fact, a 17th-century sundial. However, the fine village street, with its sundial, is only part of the attraction of Great Staughton.

A short distance to the west of the main street you will find The Town, where, grouped around 13th-century St Andrew's church, are a number of attractive old dwellings. The dominant building is Place House, built around 1540, gaunt but impressive behind its high brick wall and now only a third of its original size. See also, next to the church, Robin Hood

The White Hart Inn, a 16th-century coaching inn on the road from Cambridge to the Midlands, with the typical passage for the coaches to go through into the yard, has a small restaurant as well as the long bar which opens onto the inn yard. The menu includes various steaks, pork chops, a selection of vegetarian meals, half-a-chicken and more. There is a raft of steamed puddings to choose from, and home-made apple pie, bread and butter pudding and pancakes. Telephone: 01480 860345.

The Tickled Trout restaurant and bar is situated by the edge of Grafham Water, overlooking the lake at Mander Park, West Perry. Snacks and meals are served here.

Cottage. This was once a pub, one of many in the village, with a maltings and a brewery next door to it. From a gap next to the cottage a delightful series of half-hidden gabled buildings, retreating from the road, can be seen.

The walk takes you across fields to Grafham Water, a vast man-made lake where there are facilities for many recreational pursuits, passing Mander Park, with its nature reserve and visitor centre. For anyone finding the walk to Grafham Water too strenuous, a short walk to The Town, passing the church and Place House, is recommended.

THE WALK

❶ From the main street and the sundial go west, and where the B645 swings right, go straight ahead along The Causeway, the road to the church. After passing a field on the right, reach a seat by a footpath sign on the right, under a row of chestnut trees.

❷ If you have time, and certainly for the short village walk, go straight on for ½ mile to The Town, passing the church and historic Place House on the right. Having explored the old part of the village, retrace your steps to the seat. Turn along the grassy path and where the trees on the left end, go half right and then swing left to pass a hedge on the right. Follow it round to the right and continue diagonally across a cinder car park out to a road junction at a bend.

❸ If you are taking the short village walk, turn right and return to the sundial.

Continuing the full walk, take the road almost opposite, towards Grafham Water and walk straight down the road for nearly ½ mile. At the cross-roads near the hamlet of Dillington, go left on a minor road.

❹ Just before a wood on the left go right at some white gates, on a wide farm track. After passing a track off half-left to a cottage the path swings slightly left to follow a hedge on the right. Leave the hard farm road at Agden Hill Farm, and go straight on along a grass path through a gap in the hedge and then follow a ditch and a hedge on the right which later turns to the right, towards a wood.

❺ At the corner of the wood go right along a grassy headland path, with a hedge on the right. Ahead is the wide expanse of Grafham Water. Continue on the track for ½ mile. Go under grid lines and soon swing slightly right to pick up a hardcore farm road with a hedge on the left.

Keep on the main hard track, which after passing two paths to the left, swings round to the right slightly and in 100 yards

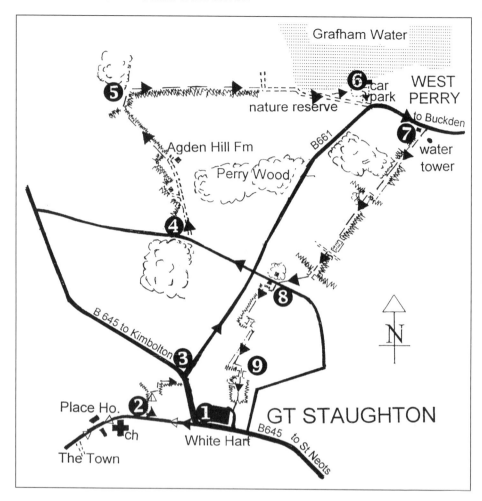

runs almost beside the water. Go through a little gate to the left near Valley Creek Hide and swing right along a gravel path, leading past a small visitor centre into a car park, beside The Tickled Trout restaurant.

❻ Walk through the car park, turn right at the end along the access track, which leads out to the road. Keep left and walk through West Perry for about ¼ mile.

❼ Just beyond the Wheatsheaf public house and almost behind a bus shelter, go right over a stile. Cross two more stiles in quick succession and keep beside a fence and hedge on the right, through a meadow on a well-used narrow path.

Go right over the stile just before reaching the wood. Then go left and continue between a hedge on the left and the wood. At the end of the wood keep straight on and at the corner of the field

Grafham Water.

go right for 50 yards and left beside a radio mast. After a small copse, continue on a headland path with a hedge on the left. When the hedge ends, go left across a culvert and walk on the opposite side of the ditch, then cross back to continue in the same direction as before, with a hedge and ditch on the left.

At the corner of the field go over a culvert and bear slightly right on a roughly diagonal cross-field path towards a point about 30 yards from the left end of a group of trees surrounding some cottages opposite. Having crossed the field, turn right along a road and in 40 yards turn left at a footpath sign.

❽   Walk beside the hedge on the right and at the corner go right, and follow the waymarked headland path. At the far

corner go left and right over a sleeper bridge, and then left again for 20 yards. Turn right and continue along the edge of a large field. At the corner go left.

❾ After about 200 yards go right skirting
the edge of the field, and then go straight
on towards the houses, crossing a ditch by
a sleeper bridge. Go straight across the
field making for the electricity pole at the
far side. A gap in the hedge beside the pole
leads to a tarmac footpath. Walk along the
footpath and then bear right to a road
junction, swing left to the main street of
Great Staughton and turn right to the sundial.

EASTON

Length: 3½ miles

Getting there: Easton is about 6 miles west of Huntingdon. Go west on the A14 and 3 miles from the A1 intersection, turn left on a minor road to Easton, ½ mile away.	Parking: There is a wide verge just opposite the church. Alternatively, kerbside parking is possible in Spaldwick and the walk can be made starting at Spaldwick church.	Map: OS Landranger – Bedford etc 153 (GR 139716).

A stream runs through the small village of Easton, on one side of which are some very old, very picturesque, houses including the black and white half-timbered Manor House, built around 1540. At intervals small footbridges link the two sides. Set by a green at one end of the village street is a fine Georgian house,

brick with a slate roof, and on an adjacent corner is the church, with a broach spire.

Easton and its larger neighbour, Spaldwick, lie in a shallow valley. The land to the south rises gently to about 100 ft. This pleasant walk follows a well-used track to Spaldwick and after a circuit of the village

FOOD and DRINK

The George at Spaldwick is only a mile away. Built before 1584, it opened as a pub in 1676, a coaching inn on the Kettering-Cambridge-Colchester road. The menu includes lamb steak in redcurrant sauce, barbecued half-a-chicken, home-baked ham dijonaisse, and many fish and vegetarian dishes. Telephone: 01480 890293.

climbs to Stocking Barn, before returning on a lightly-trafficked road to Easton

THE WALK

❶ From the church, go west along Church Lane. Keep straight on at the junction with Chapel Lane and about 100 yards further on, at Townsend Farm, the road ends in a hard standing.

❷ Go straight on along a grassy lane with a hedge on the right. A sign indicates that this is part of the Three Shires Way. In ½ mile there is a junction with a farm road on the left which leads towards Stocking Barn. The walk will return to this point later.

❸ Continue straight on along a hard farm track with a hedge on the right and at the corner follow the track round to the right. Soon there are hedges on both sides and eventually the lane comes out at Spaldwick.

❹ Turn left towards the George. Look out on the right, as you pass, for an attractive bronze map of the village commemorating the Silver Jubilee of Queen Elizabeth II. Beyond the George, walk past the chest-

The George, at Spaldwick.

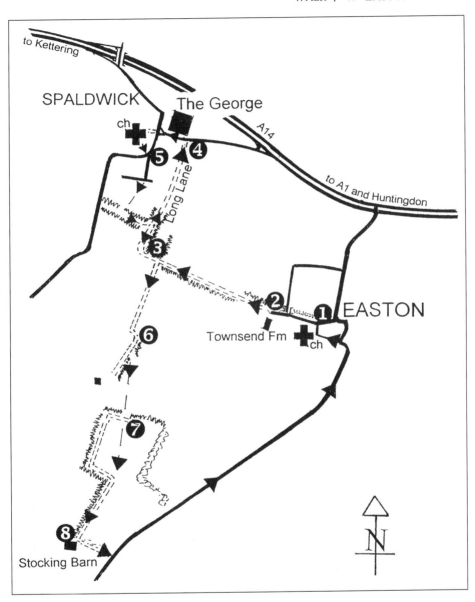

nut trees in the middle of the road, and cross Stow Road to go along narrow Church Lane into the churchyard of St James' church. The exceedingly tall spire is 152 ft high. Swing left, pass the south porch and leave the churchyard by a stile on the southern side into a meadow. Bear right at first, then go left passing a pond, to a corner of the field and through a kissing-gate to a road at a bend.

❺ Cross straight over and walk along Royston Avenue. Cross Ferriman Road and follow a grass path beside a school with a hedge on the left. Cross a stile into a field and continue in the same direction as before to a stile which can just be seen in the hedge opposite. Go through a thin belt of trees and turn left on a footpath between hedges. On reaching Long Lane, where you were earlier, turn right along the lane, following a hedge on the left. In about 200 yards turn left, still on the track. In 100 yards, at a junction, turn sharp right along a hard farm track. (For anyone wishing to return direct to Easton, go straight on at this point, retracing your steps.)

❻ In a little under ¼ mile the track makes a gradual bend round to the left and then a slightly sharper bend to the right, where a ditch comes in obliquely from the left. Just after this point leave the track, going half left across a culvert through a gap in a hedge. From here follow a cross-field path towards the mid-point of the southern hedge.

PLACES of INTEREST

On the north-eastern shore of **Grafham Water**, 4 miles away, is an Exhibition Centre and café, from where cycles may be hired. There is an 8 mile cycle route around the perimeter of the lake. Telephone: 01480 812154 for details. **Huntingdon**, a pleasant small town, with a museum in the former school attended by Oliver Cromwell, is only 6 miles away.

---

❼ At the far side of the field go through a gap in the hedge and continue in the same direction, going towards the end of a tall hedge which can be seen on the left, almost at the top of the field.

Further up the hill make for the left hand corner of a hedge which comes into view at the top. On reaching the hedge corner, join a headland farm track and keep straight on with a hedge on the right, to Stocking Barn.

❽ Turn left at the barn for 200 yards, out to a road. Go left along the road down into Easton. At the edge of the village take the first junction, left, back to the church.

ALCONBURY WESTON

Length: 3½ miles

Getting there: Alconbury Weston is a mile from the Great North Road (A1). Take the junction ½ mile north of the Alconbury interchange (where the A1 joins the northern spur of the A14). In a mile turn right opposite the White Hart to reach the village centre.

Parking: There is a small amount of street-parking alongside the brook. For customers at the White Hart there is a generous car park.

Map: OS Landranger – Peterborough 142 (GR 178769).

A major feature of Alconbury Weston is the Alconbury Brook, which rises just over the county boundary in Northamptonshire and flows south-east to join the Great Ouse near Huntingdon. The village straddles the brook and two footbridges and a ford link the two sides. Ducks constantly observe the comings and goings, humans can do likewise from a bench in the shade of the tree by the ford.

Facing each other across the ford are white Chestnut Farm, with its plain-tiled mansard roof, and white Brookside with its oriel window beneath a pentice board, looking out across a small green. The White Hart Inn at the eastern end of the

FOOD and DRINK

The White Hart has stood here since 1854. The broad fronted pub, with a wide bar, also has a family room half-hidden behind the huge fireplace. On the menu are various steaks, mixed grill, gammon and egg, chicken supreme in a white wine sauce, home-made steak and kidney pie and cajun chicken. Telephone: 01480 890331.

village, on the road called Vinegar Hill, stands next to Church Way. There is no church in the village, but Church Way leads across the fields, beside the brook, to the church at Alconbury, with its broach spire.

This walk takes you along quiet field paths to the tiny isolated village of Upton. The return is along a bridleway, crossing the little Alconbury Brook, and the walk then follows the brook back to the village.

THE WALK

❶ From the ford, go away from the village along the road with the river on the left. Pass a wooden footbridge over the river and shortly afterwards the road bears round to the right. Pass a white cottage on the right and where the road swings left, go right at a footpath sign, alongside a white cottage (No 75) into a narrow green lane for 100 yards, over a plank bridge and beside a large steel barn, into the corner of a field.

❷ Bear slightly left, in the direction of the waymark, and cross the field. At the far side swing right on to a grassy cart track, which leads to the entrance to the next field.

The White Hart Inn at Alconbury Weston.

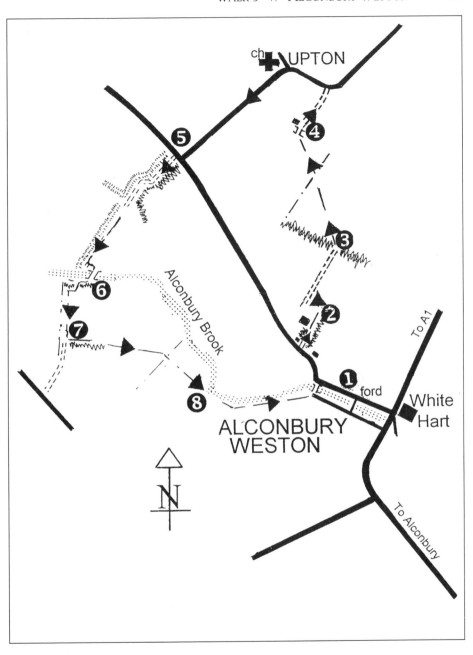

PLACES of INTEREST

Three miles north-west of Alconbury Weston is **Hamerton Wildlife Centre**, home to over 120 species of animals from all over the world. It is open daily, except Christmas Day, from 10.30 am to 6 pm (4 pm in winter). Telephone: 01832 23362.

Archers Wood which dates back to medieval times is managed by the Woodland Trust. Its wide rides attract butterflies and birds and there are many wild flowers. It is 3½ miles to the north at grid reference 173814. Go towards Hamerton and take the second turning right.

❸ Here the route goes half-left to a stile in the fence at the left side of the field. Cross the stile and continue across the next field to a stile at the foot of a tall ash tree. Continue in the same direction as before towards the roof of a house on the far side of the field. Cross a small timber bridge and then stride a low brick wall and descend a brick step to cross the orchard of Maple Tree House through a gate into a surfaced lane.

❹ Go northwards along the lane to a junction at a bend and then turn left. In 200 yards bear left beside Upton church, and walk through the village to reach, in ¼ mile, a T-junction.

❺ Turn right for 20 yards and then left onto a hard farm track with a hedge on the left and a ditch on the right. The track makes a dog-leg right and left, following the hedge. Soon the hard track ends at a corner of a field. Here swing rightish for about 10 yards and continue in the same direction on a grassy path, following a ditch on the right. At the far side of the field swing left and cross a stream on a substantial bridge.

❻ Swing right along a narrow footpath through a small uncultivated area leading through a gap in a hedge, into a large field. Turn right and continue for 100 yards along the headland. Go left on a headland path beside a fence on the right.

❼ At the corner of the field leave the bridleway and turn left on a headland path with a hedge on the right. After a stag-headed ash tree, keep straight on along a crop division which leads, on the far side, through a steel gate into a pasture. Keep straight on to a gate at a corner of the field and in 20 yards cross a stile.

❽ Follow the river bank, crossing three stiles en route. Shortly you will come to a footbridge. Turn left, cross the river and turn right back to your start.

BUCKDEN

Length: 4½ miles

Getting there: Buckden is 4 miles north of St Neots and a bit south-west of Huntingdon. Make for the interchange between the A1 and the A14, just west of Huntingdon. Go south on the A1 for about	3 miles and at a roundabout take the first exit. Parking: In the village street at the northern end of the village, beside the high brick wall, there is quite a bit of parking. For	customers there is parking in the yard of the Lion Hotel. Map: OS Landranger – Bedford etc 153 (GR192675).

Once an important staging post for coaches travelling along the Great North Road, Buckden, having been bypassed by the A1, is quieter now. Within the high brick crenellated walls fronting the street lies Buckden Towers, which from 1186 to 1842 was the palace of the Bishops of Lincoln, and was where Catherine of Aragon, the first wife of Henry VIII, was imprisoned. Its turreted buildings, enclosing a large inner courtyard with immaculate gardens, are now a retreat and a conference centre. Beyond the Towers can be seen the church of St Mary, with its parapet spire.

FOOD and DRINK

The Lion Hotel, in the High Street, is a 15th-century listed building. In the Great Hall, where you can take your coffee or afternoon tea, is the original 15th-century fireplace. The oak-panelled restaurant can offer steaks, home-made lasagne, chicken Kiev, fisherman's pie and vegetarian tartlets among a host of other options. Telephone: 01480 810313. The Pomegranate Tearooms, in the inner courtyard of Buckden Palace, are open in the afternoons on Saturdays, Sundays and Bank Holidays throughout the summer.

Close by, among other old attractive buildings in the village, is a delightful four-bay, cream-washed house with a pedimented doorway and an elegant elliptical window high in the gable.

The walk is along grassy headland paths and through pleasant woodland to cross several arms of the river Great Ouse, close to Offord lock. After leaving Offord Cluny church the walk returns to Buckden, passing Buckden marina.

THE WALK

❶ From the road junction by the Lion Hotel, take the road eastwards, passing the church on the left. Turn right into Manor Gardens and keep on the road to pass the library and then walk along a cul-de-sac. At the end, a signed path runs into an area beside a small lake. Turn right and after passing the end of the lake, keep on a tarmac path towards a housing estate. The path leads to the head of a cul-de-sac.

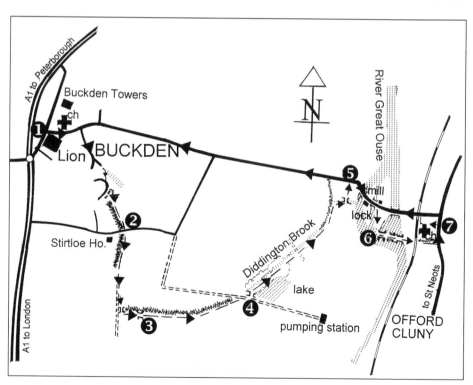

The gatehouse at Buckden Towers.

Turn left on Cranfield Way and pass a road off to the right, but keep on and bend round to the right for a few yards. Go left at a sign beside the bungalow No 66 and up a few steps and turn right on the tarmac path. Where the houses end, keep on along a headland path with a hedge on the right, to the hamlet of Stirtloe.

❷ Cross the road and go straight on along a headland path with a hedge on the right. Ahead and to the left you can see a number of lakes which border the river Ouse, a mile away. Looking through an orchard on the right, you may see the ivy-clad frontage of Stirtloe House. By a seat reach a gravel track, keep straight on and cross a footbridge beside the track. At a footpath sign turn left along a broad head-land path with a hedge on the left.

❸ Soon cross a wooden footbridge and continue beside the hedge which eventually bends half-left, and in under ¼ mile you reach a tarmac road which leads to a large brick building on the right. This is the Anglian Water Pumping Station which pumps water from the river Great Ouse up to fill the Grafham Water reservoir.

❹ Cross the road and, at a sign, cross a footbridge leading to a pleasant woodland path beside a lake, girt with bulrushes. On the left of the path is Diddington Brook, a tiny stream. Pass the end of the lake and keep on the path through the woods. If you look to the right you may see the spire of Offord D'Arcy church.

Cross a gravel track and then a stile and continue beside a hedge, on a broad grassy headland. In about 200 yards swing to the right, to follow a narrow stream on the left. In 150 yards turn left over a wooden footbridge and cross a small meadow to a stile and out to a narrow road.

❺ Turn right along the road and carefully cross a narrow bridge over the river Great Ouse and pass beside the rather derelict Offord and Buckden Mills building. Cross another bridge and immediately go right on a footpath beside Offord lock.

❻ Keep on the path which leads across several bridges, to a meadow on the east side of the river. Go through a kissing-gate and then a stile and, complying with the pedestrian traffic signals, cross the four tracks of the main London to York railway line. Walk through a field, passing on the left Offord Cluny church, and go over a stile into a lane. Turn left at a road opposite thatched Brown Bonnet Cottage.

❼ In about 50 yards turn left to All Saints' church and at the west end of the churchyard go out through a path at the corner. Walk beside the railway, through a kissing-gate to the road and turn left over the level crossing. Walk along the road, over the several arms of the river, passing beside Buckden Marina, back to Buckden.

ABBOTSLEY

Length: 5 miles (or 4 miles)

Getting there: From the Caxton Gibbet roundabout, where the A428 (Cambridge to Bedford) road crosses the A1198 (Huntingdon to Royston) road, go west along the A428 towards St Neots and take the second turning left, signed B1040	Biggleswade, and in 2 miles go right to Abbotsley. From the St Neots direction, take the B1046 to Abbotsley. **Parking:** There is room for a few cars by the red telephone box between the church and the	Jolly Abbot pub. Alongside the pub there is plenty of customer car parking. **Map:** OS Landranger – Bedford etc 153 (GR 226566).

This his pretty village is set on the slope of a hill, with houses grouped around the triangle formed by High Street, Blacksmith's Lane and High Green. The Jolly Abbot pub and St Margaret's church next door, stand above a green which slopes away down to the lower end of the High Street and the St Neots road. At the top of the green is a seat on which to sit and relax and watch the comings and goings in the village. In the fields alongside the Pitsdean Road you can see deer roaming.

Built largely of brown carstone, the church of St Margaret of Antioch, surrounded by old limes and horse chestnut trees, is unusual in that although the chancel is regularly used for worship still, the nave and tower are maintained by the Redundant Churches Trust. Atop the tower stand four statues.

This easy walk takes you along a good farm drive to Caldecote Manor, with fine views over the Bedfordshire plain, and then through narrow, leafy Hail Lane. After crossing a golf course, along the route of a Roman road it returns on a well-used headland path.

THE WALK

❶ From the village green go west along the B1046 towards St Neots. In about 200 yards turn right along a concrete farm road, following the sign to Hail Lane.

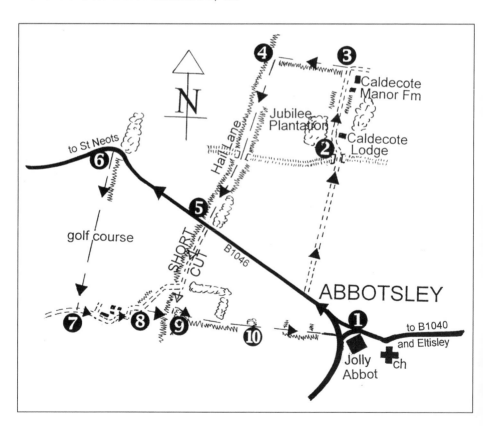

One of Abbotsley's attractive houses.

❷ In just over ½ mile, cross a bridge and a cattle grid and continue along the concrete track across a field, passing Caldecote Lodge on the right. As you climb the hill ahead look back at Abbotsley.

After crossing a third cattle grid, enter a lane which leads to Caldecote Manor Farm. Keep straight on, passing all the farm buildings on the right, ending with a brick cottage.

❸ Where the farm track bends right, turn left along a broad headland, with a hedge on the left. Ahead is a fine view westwards over the Bedfordshire plain.

❹ At the corner of the field go left down Hail Lane, a grassy track with a hedge on the right. In about 200 yards the track becomes a narrow green lane with hedges on both sides. The path swings right and left to cross a culvert and in a further ¼ mile, you reach a road.

For the shorter 4 mile walk go straight on along a grassy-middled cart track, beside a hedge on the right. Pass the end of Long Plantation, a wood on the left and where the cart track bends right towards the golf course, keep straight on along a grassy headland path. About 50 yards beyond an electricity pole on the left the headland path bends half-left and rejoins the main walk at 9 below.

PLACES of INTEREST

The market town of **St Neots**, beside the river Great Ouse, is approximately 5 miles away. There are attractive waterside gardens to wander in and from which to take boat trips.

❺ For the full 5 mile walk go right, along the road. After passing a pair of brick cottages on the left, continue along the road round some bends.

❻ On reaching a row of mature trees on the right, go left along a wide grassy path with a hedge on the left. When you reach the golf course, keeping a watchful eye to avoid being in a player's line of fire, go straight on. There are a few helpful waymarks en route.

❼ At the far side of the golf course you come out on a concrete track: turn left. Where a sign directs left to Abbotsley Golf Course and Hotel, go straight on, to pass Horseman's Cottage on the left, and continue on the concrete track through more golf course land. The concrete track ends and there is a gravel drive, passing some hotel buildings on the left. Keep to the waymarked track which bends left and then right.

❽ After a small pond on the right, leave the gravel path where it swings left, and go straight ahead, across the grass, to a waymark at the edge of the golf course. Follow a cross-field path roughly along the line of overhead electricity wires.

❾ Tunnel through a thick hedge of blackthorn and go left for a few yards and then right on a grassy headland path with a hedge on the right. This is where the shorter walk rejoins the route. Go through a wide gap in the cross-hedge and continue with the hedge on the right. When the hedge ends go straight ahead, passing a small wood on the left.

❿ Continue on a cross-field path, still following a line of electricity wires, towards Abbotsley church seen in the distance. Go through a gap into the next field, and continue with the hedge on the right. At the corner of the field cross a stile, and continue through rough ground parallel to the field boundary on the right. Soon enter the recreation ground by a stile and cross the field to a road. Walk up the tarmac road and swing left, back to the village green.

GUILDEN MORDEN

Length: 4 miles (or 2½ miles)

Getting there: Follow the A505 from Royston towards Baldock. Two miles beyond the roundabout on the western side of Royston turn right for Ashwell station and The Mordens. Go through Steeple Morden and in ½ mile turn left. Then turn left at Guilden Morden church.

Parking: For customers there is ample parking beside the Three Tuns, otherwise there are scattered places to park on-street in the village.

Map: OS Landranger – Bedford etc 153 (GR 278436).

Tucked into the south-west corner of Cambridgeshire are the twin villages of Guilden Morden and Steeple Morden, just a mile apart. This is a farming area, close to the source of the river Cam (sometimes called the Rhee) which flows north-east-ward towards Cambridge. To the south of the village, the land rises gradually towards the chalk downs of Hertfordshire.

One gets an impression, because of the number of large old farmhouses in and around the village, that agriculture in this area, at least in the past, has prospered. Many of these older buildings, both large and small, have been attractively modernized, fitting in well in this small village. Less than 5 miles away is the railway station where electric commuter trains whisk residents to their businesses in the towns of north Hertfordshire.

Among the attractive houses in the village is a pink house, now private, with the old pargetted inn-sign of The Six Bells. In the road leading to the church is a charming terrace of cottages, Avenell Terrace, and neighbouring Somborne Cottage.

The walk goes north from Guilden Morden along leafy Cobbs Lane to a footbridge over the river Cam, which leads to the neighbouring village of Tadlow. The return is along well-used field paths back to the village, passing Cherry Holt, a long white house with dormer windows buried deep in the thatch, and a straw peacock standing on the thatched porch.

THE WALK

❶ From the Three Tuns cross the road and go along the bridleway opposite, a green lane between hedges which comes out to the corner of a broad field, and continue with a hedge on the right. Follow the main grass track which swings left

passing an electricity pole to join an estate road heading to the church.

❷ At the end cross the village street, turn right and walk through the churchyard passing the south porch to a gate at the east side. Cross the road, go straight past the side of the Edward VII pub on the right and enter the recreation ground by the village hall. Continue with the fence on the left.

In the corner go left for 5 yards and then right, over a stile and continue straight across the field on a crop division. At a waymark, close to an electricity pole, bear slightly left and on a grassy sward follow a hedge, beside waymarked posts into a gravel drive and out to the road, 100 yards distance.

❸ Cross straight over and at the footpath sign go along the drive to 'Old Brickfields No 45'. Just before the house, at a waymark, turn left across a narrow strip of garden and then keep on a narrow path beside at first a ditch, and later a large pond, on the left. At the end of the garden go over a stile to a cross-field path towards the left side of a hedge opposite. When you reach the hedge corner, at a waymark, go right along a headland with a hedge on the left and at the corner go through a gap in a hedge and out to turn left along Cobbs Lane, a green lane.

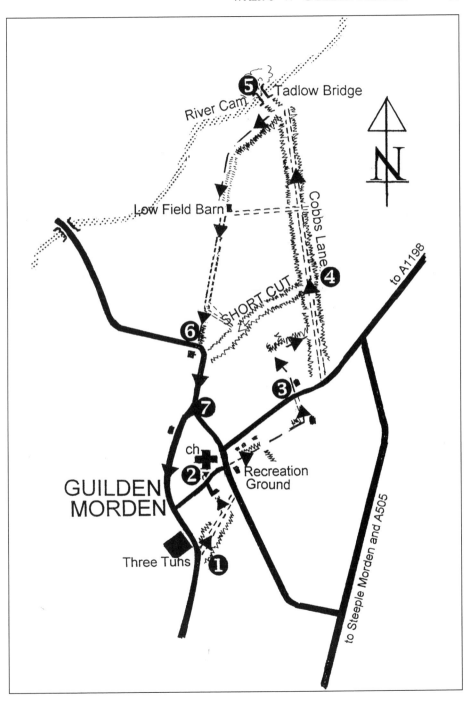

Thatched Somborne Cottage and Avenell Terrace.

❹ In just under ¼ mile, at a junction of three tracks, the green lane on the left leads back to Guilden Morden, for anyone who wants to take the short cut. Otherwise, for the full walk, bear slightly right and keep straight on in the same direction. In a further ¼ mile cross straight over a farm road which leads to Low Field Barn and continue along the green lane.

At the approach to the Cam, bear left to Tadlow Bridge. The river is quite tiny here and it seems such an isolated spot to have a substantial footbridge. No doubt Cobbs Lane was far more important in times past, perhaps before other roads were built.

❺ After having a look at the bridge turn round and retrace your steps for about 150 yards. Just before the track makes a bend to the right, at a waymark on a pole, go right on a grass headland with a hedge on the left which soon becomes a ditch. In ½ mile pass, on the left, Low Field Barn and join a farm road. Straight ahead you can see Guilden Morden church spire. When the hard farm road swings left to Little Green Farm keep straight on, on a grass track between crops at first, then with a hedge on the left.

❻ At the road go left, and in a few yards pass a farmyard where free range ornamental poultry of various sorts can be seen.

❼ At the road junction bear right along Dubbs Knoll Road. After passing the Congregational church on the left and a little seat on a green on the right, pass Church Street on the left and keep straight on to High Street to reach in 300 yards the Three Tuns.

WISTOW

Length: 5½ miles

Getting there: From the A14 grade-separated interchange west of Huntingdon follow the A141 road. Turn left to Warboys and then take the B1040 towards Ramsey. In 2 miles go left to Wistow, ½ mile away.

Parking: There is some street-side parking. Beside the Three Horseshoes pub there is plenty of customer parking.

Map: OS Landranger – Peterborough 142 (GR 278809).

Walking round the rectangle of streets which forms the centre of Wistow, one cannot but be impressed by the variety of old houses, mostly thatched, in this attractive Cambridgeshire village. At the end of Parsonage Street as you turn into Manor Street, is Manor Farm House, a broad-fronted white house with a mottled buff, plain tiled roof. Look up to the base of the chimney stack and you will see the date 1662. The painted black swags on the façade are somewhat unusual. The last house in Manor Street, on the right opposite the village hall, is Porch House, mainly white, with black shuttered windows, and part black weatherboard, all beneath very deep thatch which almost hides the five dormer windows of the upper storey.

In Bridge Street, opposite the post office, are some modern houses with interesting corbelling details in the brickwork beneath the main roof and the garage roof. At the junction of Bridge Street with Church Street is a long white house, The Shieling, with a bow window, two gabled dormers and a thatched roof, and decorative brickwork under the upper windows. Just round the bend from the Three Horseshoes, in Mill Street, is the three-storey Mill House.

The church of St John the Baptist stands on one corner of that square of roads. On the north side of the nave roof is a rather unusual turret. Some fine gargoyles, functional though they may be, ornament the roof line. Inside, in the choir, are carved wooden angels above stone corbels on which are carved people, animals and birds. The Women's Institute have contributed a wall hanging – a sampler – to commemorate 50 years 1938–1988.

This walk at the edge of the fens is along minor roads, well used footpaths and a short length of permissive path, across farmland to the small, pretty villages of

Manor Farm House dating from 1622.

Upwood and Great Raveley (pronounced to rhyme with bravely).

THE WALK

❶ Start along Parsonage Street, beside the church on the left. At the left-hand bend enter Manor Street, passing Manor Farm House, and later, the fine Porch House on the right.

❷ At the T-junction turn left along Bridge Street, and at the next T-junction turn right into Church Street. In 100 yards turn left to walk through Oaklands Avenue, passing the playing fields.

❸ In 300 yards turn right along Harris's Lane. The surfaced road ends where a track goes left to a farm. Go straight on past a wooden gate, along a grassy lane between hedges. The next ¼ mile is along a permissive path. In 100 yards the lane opens into a large field. Continue along the grassy headland path with the hedge on the right.

❹ At the end of the field cross a substantial bridge and turn left along a headland path beside a ditch on the left. Follow the ditch until a similar bridge is reached. Cross the bridge, turn right, beside the

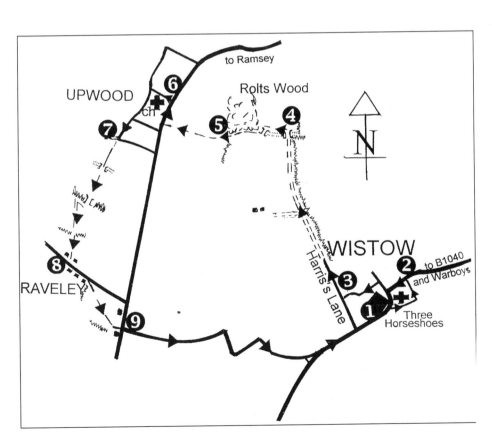

ditch, and skirt the edge of Rolts Wood on the right.

❺ When you reach the end of the wood, bear half right, cross a culvert into the next field and continue with a ditch on the right towards the village of Upwood. Go through a small pedestrian gate, out to the road and turn right.

❻ Take the first turning left to Upwood. Turn left at a T-junction, with the church on the corner (a few yards to the right is the Cross Keys pub). There are a number of picturesque cottages and houses in this street.

❼ In ¼ mile the road bends left and Meadow Lane goes off to the right. Here go straight on along a well-used footpath. At the field boundary, cross a ditch and continue on a cross-field path. At the hedge, cross a bridge and stile and go right beside a hedge. In a few yards turn left along a headland path with a barbed-wire fence on the right. Continue straight on, crossing a number of stiles to reach a road beside a letter box in Little Raveley.

❽ Turn left along the road and after passing The Pightle on the right and just by the 'Out-of-30' sign leave the road, going half-right at the footpath sign. The path goes roughly diagonally across a field. At the far side pick up a cinder track which then swings left out to a road.

❾ Cross straight over to follow the minor road signed 'Wistow 1½'. The road, after several sharp bends, leads out at a grass triangle to a T-junction. Go left, on the road back to Wistow and the start.

ELSWORTH

Length: 6 miles

Getting there: Elsworth is 8 miles west of Cambridge. Follow the A14 between Cambridge and Huntingdon and leave it at the junction for Swavesey. Follow the signs to Boxworth and Elsworth is 2 miles further on.

Parking: There is a small layby on the left of the main road, just past the turning on the left signed 'Village Only' and just before the recreation ground on the right. There is also a customers' car park at the rear of The Poacher pub.

Maps: OS Landranger – Bedford etc 153; Cambridge etc 154 (GR 315637).

Much of Elsworth lies tucked away in a narrow valley beside a tiny brook, crossed by several bridges. Picturesque thatched cottages together with modernised dwellings are ranged on both sides of the valley. On the hill above is Holy Trinity church, at the eastern end of which is a magnificent row of lime trees, a fine setting for the delicate tracery of the east window. The creator of *Thomas the Tank Engine* and other stories, the Rev Wilbert Awdry, was rector of this church from 1946 till 1953. Many of the early stories were written, originally for his small son,

FOOD and DRINK

The Poacher was built about 1650 as the brew house for the Manor. Look around you in the pub and you will see a lot of carving; outside the pub sign is not painted but carved, and the two sides are different. All this and the village sign on the verge opposite are the work of one man, Guy Soff. The pub serves such food as chicken tikka masala, lamb or chicken madras with pilau rice, breast of duckling with grand marnier and various vegetarian dishes. Telephone: 01954 267219.

in the rectory next to the church.

Near the end of the village, almost opposite The Poacher public house, is the most attractive seven-bay Manor House. At one time relatives of Oliver Cromwell, the Disbrowes, held the manor of Elsworth. The name is variously spelt Disbrowe or Desborough. A cottage in Brook Street commemorates that name.

The walk takes you to the village of Knapwell and then on good paths to the edge of Boxworth. Here if you wish you can make a diversion to see the village. The way continues past the Agricultural Research Station, along another track back to Knapwell. After returning to Elsworth church, the walk then makes a circuit beside the brook, to show you the older buildings of the village.

THE WALK

❶ Starting opposite the Manor House, close to The Poacher, walk along the road towards Boxworth. Pass Roger's Close on the left and in 50 yards turn right up The Drift, passing an entrance to the church on the right. Where the track forks, keep right on a good farm track and soon you are on a headland track with a mature hedge on the right.

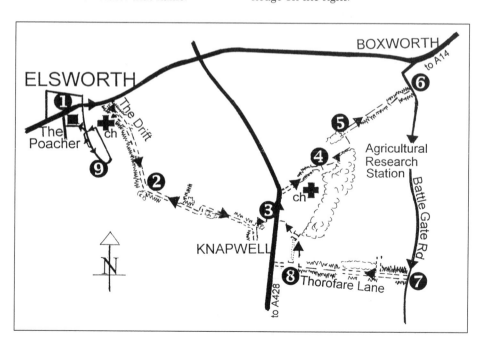

Thatched Disbrowe Cottage.

❷ At the field corner go left, and in a few yards the hedge on the right has been replaced by a newly planted hedge line. Continue on the farm track which passes a small wooded area on the left and then makes a dog leg left and right, passing a hedge on the right. Go under the grid wires and soon walk beside a hedge on the left. Leave the cinder track where it makes a sharp turn to the right towards some farm buildings. At this point go left for a few yards and swing round to the right along a field edge. Almost immediately cross a stile under a hawthorn bush, into a narrow pasture. Walk down the field and at the end turn left, keeping beside the fence which soon makes a right turn. In about 50 yards go over a stile to Knapwell.

❸ Turn left along the road for just over ¼

mile. Go right along a lane signed 'Public Footpath Boxworth', beside some horse chestnut trees. Pass Knapwell church on the right, continuing to the end of the lane, by a house. Go straight on through a low steel squeezer stile, into an attractive narrow path between high ornamental hedges which leads to a steel kissing-gate and a timber footbridge.

❹ After the bridge go left for 2 yards and climb a bank to cross two stiles in close succession, into a grass field. Bear half right towards the wood on the right. Cross another stile and turn left on a narrow path between the wood and a fence on the left. Cross a stile and immediately turn left across the field, passing the edge of a small wood on the left.

PLACES of INTEREST

To get to **Hilton Turf Maze**, go west towards Papworth and in 2 miles turn right. In a further mile, on the edge of Hilton, bear right. The turf maze is on the left about ¼ mile beyond the junction.

❺ Go over a further stile and turn right along a well-maintained headland path. After crossing a concrete farm track keep straight along a grassy path with a hedge on the right. Swing right through the hedge, at a waymark, into the corner of a field. Cross a stile into a narrow field and walk straight on over another stile out to a road.

If you wish to make a detour, go left along the road for ¼ mile and you will reach Boxworth, and the Golden Ball public house.

❻ To continue the walk, go right along Battle Gate Road, a lightly trafficked cul de sac. Pass on the right the Agricultural Research Station (ADAS) and in a further ½ mile pass the track to High Barns.

❼ In less than ¼ mile turn right off the road on a hard track with hedges on both sides, known as Thorofare Lane On the left, just after entering the lane, is a Forestry Commission Research Plot.

Keep on the lane. There are woods on the right. Later the lane becomes grassy with mature hedges on both sides, and starts gradually to descend. At the bottom, and just before the lane crosses a narrow watercourse, go right on a grass footpath, (if you reach a small brick pumping station on the left you have gone too far).

❽ In a few yards the path comes out to a large field. Continue on the headland, stream and trees on the left. At the field corner go left and cross a footbridge into a meadow. Follow the waymarks, pass an ancient pollarded tree and cross a stile in the far hedge leading to a narrow path which comes out to a road in Knapwell.

Go right for a few yards and then left over a stile. You are now on the path that brought you from Elsworth. Return, crossing the stile under the hawthorn tree and swing left to the hard farm track, and turn right. Keep on the track till you reach the white gate on the left which leads to Elsworth church. Go past the row of lime trees and Holy Trinity church and then down The Causeway.

❾ At the bottom turn left and walk beside the stream on the right. In about 300 yards cross a footbridge and return on the opposite side of the stream. Having returned to the end of The Causeway, swing left and walk along Cotterell's Lane. Turn right at the T-junction and right again to return to the start.

BENWICK

Length: 3½ miles

Getting there: From the south go to Chatteris (use the A141 or A142) and at the five-way roundabout junction on the north side of the town take the minor road to Doddington. In about a mile, cross the Forty Foot Drain and immediately turn left and follow its north bank for 2½ miles. Turn right for Benwick and at a T-junction turn right again. A sharp left bend brings you into High Street. From the north, follow the B1093 from Whittlesey.

Parking: There is a reasonable amount of parking in a short wide cul-de-sac which leads off the northern end of High Street, where the main road through the village makes a right-angle bend.

Map: OS Landranger – Peterborough 142 (GR 341905).

There are few villages as isolated as Benwick which lies in the heart of the Fens, equidistant from Chatteris, March and Ramsey, and it is this isolation which contributes to the interest of this walk. The surrounding area is intensively cultivated with a wide variety of crops. Hedges are rare, the field boundaries being deep, straight drainage ditches.

The wide, slowly flowing river through

Footbridge over the river Nene.

Benwick is the river Nene, but it is not the same river as now flows through Peterborough. It is an old course of the river which ran here before the waters were controlled, channelled and tamed, and the rivers modified. Throughout the centuries, the rivers of the fens have been changing their courses from time to time. As they meandered across the flat lands, barely higher than the sea, the flow of their waters became very slow and subject to regular tidal movements. Because of this some river beds became blocked by silt washed upstream by the tides and, to a lesser extent, by clay and chalk carried down from higher land forcing the rivers into new courses and leaving behind bands of solid silt and clay, called rodhams or roddons, which form stable land, amidst the peat.

Some of Benwick's houses in the past were built partly on a roddon and partly on the peat, and in consequence over the years tipped towards the shrinking peat, walls cracking, door and window frames askew. Most of these houses have now gone, and Benwick's houses today are solidly built.

Wandering around Benwick, from the grassy area by the river and old church-

---

FOOD and DRINK

Less than 4 miles away at Doddington is the Three Tuns public house which serves food. It is an old coaching house and reputedly has a ghost, that of a previous landlady some 350 years ago. Meals include butterfly breast of chicken, rump steak, mixed grill, chicken cordon bleu, moussaka and lasagne. Telephone: 01354 740220.

yard, where there is a bench by the river from which to watch the ducks, to the southern end of the High Street beyond the Five Alls, you will discover quite a lot of little 'snickets' joining one road to another for walkers.

This peaceful short walk is mostly beside the old course of the Nene, then making a loop along a farm road across the rich arable land eventually to cross the river and return on the opposite bank.

THE WALK

❶ Starting at the short wide cul-de-sac, being the north end of High Street, cross the old course of the river Nene by the footbridge and immediately turn left along a riverside footpath. Note, in passing, on the right a churchyard within which is the 'Site of Parish Church of St Mary the Virgin 1850–1980'.

With the river on the left, pass several houses and later, just after Nene Cottage on the right, swing right, away from the river to turn left at a road.

❷ The road swings back towards the river. Walk if possible along the verge beside the river. In a little over ¼ mile reach a bridge over the river opposite a road which leads to Keyworth House Farm.

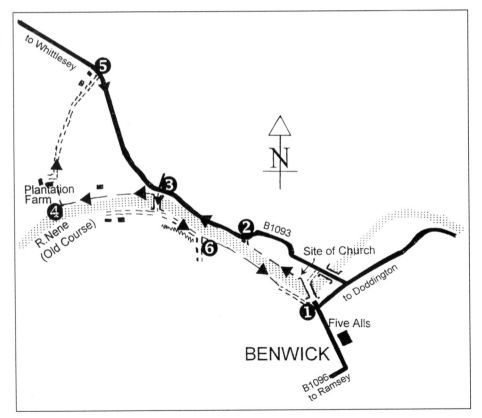

❸ Go left towards the bridge for about 50 yards and then turn right beside a Second World War brick pillbox, on a narrow path which leads to the river bank. In ¼ mile pass a track off to the right leading to a group of corrugated iron and wood sheds. Keep on for a further ¼ mile beside the river on the left to just beyond a bend to the left.

❹ At a waymark, turn right away from the river, along a crop division. Pass, on the left, a group of sheds and come out to a hard farm road. Go straight ahead. On the skyline, half-left, you can see the tall chimneys of the brickworks in the Peterborough area.

Bob under a gate and here the track is surfaced. Pass a couple of houses on the left and shortly come out to a road close to a cream-washed chalet bungalow on the left.

❺ Turn right and walk back towards Benwick. When you reach the point where you left the road, turn right and go over the bridge and immediately after, go left along a cart track, with the river on the left.

❻ Keep beside the river where the cart track turns right, and continue on a grassy path which comes out to a narrow surfaced road beside some bushes on the right, leading in a few yards back to High Street and the start.

HOLYWELL

Length: 5 miles

Getting there: Holywell is 2 miles east of St Ives. Turn off the A14 at the A1096 intersection for St Ives. After crossing the Great Ouse turn right at the third roundabout on the A1123 and in a mile go right for Needingworth. Turn right in the middle of the village on a minor road signed for Holywell. In a mile turn left to the Old Ferry Boat Inn.

Parking: There is a small area beside the river in front of the Old Ferry Boat Inn where cars are parked, but the inn has a large customer car park at the rear.

Maps: OS Landranger – Bedford etc 153; Cambridge etc 154 (GR 342706).

Holywell is a charming village on the banks of the river Great Ouse. Terns swoop and dive over the river, boats come and go and thatched houses abound in a series of chocolate box pictures alongside the river. Some of the houses are very old; one has the date 1623 imprinted on its chimney base. As there is only one road into and out of the village it remains very quiet.

Just below the church is the well that gives the village its name. In early July the villagers 'dress' the well, creating, with hundreds of flower heads and leaves, pictures representing some text or hymn line.

The Old Ferry Boat Inn at the far end of the village is mainly thatched, and it dates back to AD 980 at least; it is probably the oldest inn in Britain. There is evidence to suggest that an alehouse was here as far back as the 6th century. The inn has a ghost, one Juliet Tousley, who died after a broken love affair 900 years ago. She lies resting beneath a granite gravestone in the main bar.

The walk takes you to the historic market town of St Ives, starting alongside the river and reaching the old St Ives Bridge, upon which stands an ancient chapel. The return is through the town and along a well used leafy path.

THE WALK
❶ From the river, outside the Old Ferry Boat Inn, follow the Ouse Valley Way westward along the road, passing many thatched cottages on the right, until you reach the church on the left. Low down on the left, just within the churchyard is the well.

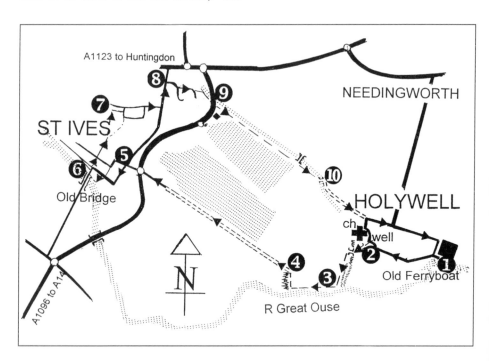

St Ives bridge, with its ancient chapel.

❷ Immediately before the churchyard go left over a stile, walking to a stile beside the dilapidated gate, and cross a concrete cart bridge. Keep in the same direction across a meadow and at the hedge, cross a long footbridge and a stile, and swing left to go parallel to a ditch on the left. Go through a sparse cross-hedge.

❸ At the river's edge, turn right beside the river on the left. In 200 yards, at a cross-hedge, go right for about 20 yards and cross a stile, then continue beside the river. At the next cross-hedge, go right, away from the river and in 200 yards go left over a ditch to join a wide gravel road with hedges on both sides.

❹ Walk for a mile down the gravel road, which becomes a tarmac road edged with

gravel pits, to reach St Ives. At the roundabout cross straight over and walk down Meadow Lane, to pass Needingworth Road on the right.

❺ In 50 yards turn left and walk into the town centre. After passing the car park and bus station on the left turn right into the market square. Pass Cromwell's statue and turn left beside St Ives Free Church, down a little footpath to the river Ouse. Go right and walk the promenade beside the river to the historic St Ives bridge.

❻ Do not go over the bridge, but go right. When you come to the end of the street go left a few yards and then right through an archway beside the post office. Soon cross a road at a Pelican crossing, go left a few yards and then right along

Crown Walk. This little street ends at a footpath leading to a park. Keep beside a terrace of houses on the left and the park on the right.

❼ At the end of the park you come to a T-junction of tracks. Here turn right on a tarmac track and then at the first opportunity turn left, leaving the park. At a road bear left and in 50 yards turn right along Fairfields. Walk 300 yards to the end and turn left for 300 yards to the second road on the right.

❽ Turn right into Sheepfolds and after a bend right past Elsworth Close, go left into Rookery Close. Where the close swings round to the right, bear left on a tarmac footpath which leads to a bridge across a ditch. Turn right, on a grassy path between hedges.

❾ The path comes out to the main road on a bend. Carefully cross straight over. On the other side of the road go through a kissing-gate on a footpath beside a wide ditch on the left and a very new looking building on the right. Go through another kissing-gate and cross a public footpath at right-angles. Notice, on the right, a large lake. At the end of the lake on the right, climb concrete steps, cross a track leading to a Bailey bridge, then down again. A little further on there is another lake on the right.

❿ Cross the ditch on a timber bridge and then turn right and continue with the ditch on the right. The footpath leads to a gravel track passing The Pastures on the right, and comes out to a road at a bend. Go straight on, ignore the turning to the left, and in ¼ mile bend round to the right and back to the Old Ferry Boat.

BARRINGTON

Length: 5½ miles (or 4 miles)

Getting there: Barrington is 7 miles south west of Cambridge. From Junction 10 on the M11, take the A10 towards Royston. In 3½ miles, at Foxton station turn right and in 1½ miles, reach a T-junction at Barrington

village green. For the Royal Oak, go left for about ½ mile.

Parking: There is a small parking area at the eastern end of the green, directly opposite the road to Foxton. The Royal

Oak has its own customer car park.

Map: OS Landranger – Cambridge etc 154 (GR 396498).

The magnificent greens of Barrington are a surprise and a delight to see. One is ¾ mile long and extensive, dominated by All Saints' church on a slight rise. The other, quite large green is across the road by the post office. The village has many beautiful old houses, a well-cared for cricket pitch and seats are dotted around the green. Geese and ducks congregate at the western end.

Inside the church, at the foot of the tower, are set out the Tower Rules for the bell ringers, dated 1876. One rule states that: 'Drinking, smoking, loud and boister-

FOOD and DRINK

The Royal Oak is a large, half-timbered 14th century house standing back from the road. The scope of the menu is wide: beef and oyster pie, Royal game pie, tagliatelle marinara, Barrington hotpot and rack of English lamb are just a few of the dishes. Telephone: 01223 870791.

ous talking or jesting and above all disputing, are most unseemly among God's ministers in His house and are hereby forbidden in this belfry.'

A branch of the river Cam, called the Rhee, flows through a broad valley northeastwards towards Cambridge. Barrington lies on the north bank of the river and the land rises gradually to a small chalk down. This walk is along pleasant well-used paths, climbing the hill to the north of the village and descending the other side to Harlton. From the hill are fine wide views to the south across the broad valley. To the north you can see, a mile away, the dish aerials of the University of Cambridge's Radio Astronomy Observatory.

THE WALK

❶ Starting just south of the church, at the junction with the road to Foxton, walk west across the green, passing the children's playground on the right. At a corner of the green opposite a white cottage, No 2, bear right on a surfaced road.

❷ In about 100 yards, at a footpath sign, go right over a stile to a lovely, well-walked headland path with a hedge on the right.

❸ The broad track you are on shortly swings right. Here the official path continues along a narrow headland with the hedge on the right. However, local people seem to continue along the broad track which runs along the other side of the hedge, rejoining the official route just before Wilsmere Down Farm. The hedge on the left ends and the grass track swings slightly left, passing the farm and, on the right, some newly planted trees.

❹ Having passed the farm, reach a hard farm road at right angles. Cross over and continue on a broad grass track with a ditch on the left, up to Long Plantation, a narrow belt of woodland. Turn right on the grass path and continue round the wood on your left. There is a wide view to the right now as you climb this small hill. At the end of the wood swing left and continue, now with a tall hedge on the left, up to a wood at the top of the hill. There is a choice of routes at this point.

❺ For those not visiting Harlton, following the shorter walk, go straight on across a sleeper bridge into the wood and bear left on a path through this narrow wood for about ¼ mile to rejoin the walk at the end of the wood.

For the main walk to Harlton, do not enter the wood but turn right at a sign, and continue along a headland path with the wood on left. At the corner of the field, at a sign, go left through the tree-belt and then descend on a grass headland path with a hedge on the right. Half-right you can see a dish aerial of the Radio Astronomy Observatory.

❻ On reaching the opposite side of the

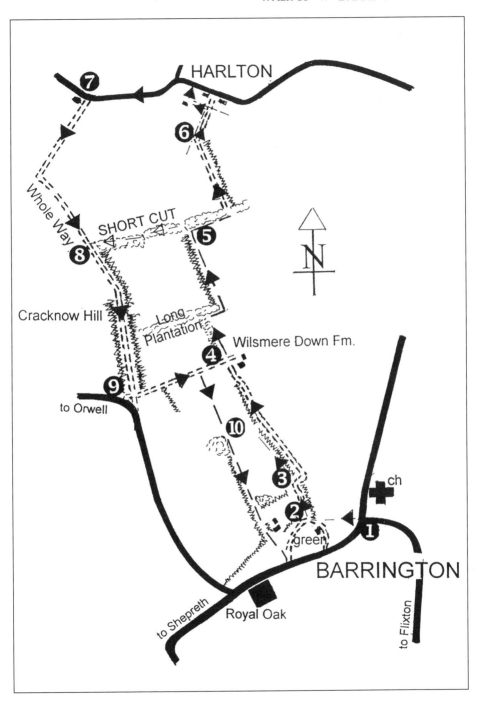

The village post office and horse trough at Barrington.

field, bear half-right and continue with a fence on the left. At the end of the field do NOT continue along a track into the farm yard, but turn left over a stile into a pasture with a fence on the right. In about 100 yards, close to a brick barn, go right at a waymark through a squeezer stile and continue out to the road, High Street, at Harlton. Turn left along the road. After passing a pond on the right, keep left on Eversden Road.

7 At the end of the village, where the road swings right past a white thatched cottage, go half-left along a broad farm road, called Whole Way. In about ¼ mile the track makes a right-angled turn to the left and you climb the slight hill. Near the top of the hill pass, on the left, the end of a long belt of woodland. It is here that the

short cut avoiding Harlton rejoins the main walk.

8 Continue on a grass track beside a hedge on the left. At the top of the hill, with wide views ahead, go straight on down a fine wide green lane.

9 Just before reaching a road at a bend, turn left on a farm drive going towards Wilsmere Down Farm. Pass a cross-hedge on the right and continue on the track then, in nearly 200 yards, turn right at a waymark, along a cross-field path.

10 At the far side of the field pass on the right a plantation of young trees, cross a ditch and then continue along a broad headland path with a wood on the right. At the end of the field pass a young

The delightful 14th-century Royal Oak inn.

PLACES of INTEREST

One of the National Trust's most important estates, **Wimpole Hall**, is 5 miles away. The adjacent **Home Farm** has the largest rare breeds centre in East Anglia. Telephone: 01223 207257. **Fowlmere Nature Reserve**, 4 miles south of Barrington, has a nature trail and bird hide. Telephone: 01767 680551.

Duxford, the home of Europe's biggest collection of historic aircraft, also has tanks, military vehicles, D-Day displays, and flight simulations. It can be found just 4 miles from Barrington at the M11/A505 junction. Telephone: 01223 835000.

plantation on the left. Keep straight on, go through a cross-hedge and continue on a headland path, hedge on the right.

At the next corner follow a narrow path between hedges, to pass the cricket pavilion, and come out on Barrington Green. Turn left and walk along the edge of the green, back to the church.

UPWELL

Length: 2 miles

Getting there: Use the A1101, a winding road between Ely and Wisbech. Upwell is about 5 miles south of Wisbech. Coming from Ely, pass the village of Three Holes and in 2 miles the

Five Bells is just by Church Bridge where the road makes a sharp right turn.

Parking: There is some on-street parking alongside the

river. There is plenty of parking for customers beside the Five Bells pub.

Map: OS Landranger – Ely etc 143 (GR 505027).

The area around Wisbech is noted for fruit growing and there are many orchards in and around Upwell; it is particularly attractive to see when the trees are in blossom. Another of the attractions of this long flourishing village is the river, which runs down the centre of the village. The splayed grassy banks are dotted with daffodils in spring, wild flowers and the occasional flowering cherry tree, silver birch and a few small shrubs. Wherever you look there are taller trees between and behind the houses, overtopping them.

On each side of the river runs a road

FOOD and DRINK

The Five Bells public house stands right next door to St Peter's church. The church has six bells, not five! The gleaming white Five Bells has a nautical theme: port and starboard leading lights, other brass ship's lights and a porthole decorate the pub. It serves barbecue spare ribs, pizzas, steak and kidney pie, lasagne, pasta shapes in a four-cheese sauce and much else besides. Telephone: 01945 772222.

watching the river and the world go by. A happy village.

Over the years, much work has been done in draining the fens and improving this low-lying land south and west of the Wash. The river which meanders through the village, separating Norfolk from Cambridgeshire, is the old route of the river Nene. Now the main river Nene has been straightened and improved and flows directly from Peterborough to Wisbech bypassing the great loop to the south through March and Upwell. Although the main flow is bypassed, this old river Nene is a fine looking river and gives the village an interesting and unusual setting.

This pleasant, short walk starts beside the river and loops along a field path through an orchard to a minor road,

with a variety of houses, mostly of warm brick, and in a charming juxtaposition of styles, all reflected in the usually calm water of the river. Two road bridges and a footbridge link the parallel roads. On sunny days old folk sit in their gardens with their neighbours, chatting and

The Five Bells, next to St Peter's church in Upwell.

returning along a farm road back to the river again.

THE WALK

❶ From the Five Bells, go left and walk beside the river along the Norfolk side. Cross the river on a footbridge opposite the Upwell Methodist church, then go left along the Cambridgeshire side.

❷ Pass Dodd's Stile, a cottage on the right, and immediately turn right at a footpath sign and go through a steel gate. Walk beside a ditch on the left, through an orchard with large, gnarled apple trees.

❸ Reach a road, Thurlands Drove, and turn left. Keep on this quiet road and after passing a row of semi-detached houses,

walk about 200 yards further and turn left down a farm track with a mature hedge on the left and a ditch on the right at first. Squeeze beside an iron gate, and keep straight on passing a house, Strawberry House, on the right. The path veers slightly to the left and runs between orchards.

❹ Shortly reach a road and turn left beside the river. Pass Hall Bridge, leading across the river to School Road and the Globe Inn, but continue straight on beside the river to cross back at the next road bridge, to the Five Bells close to the church and the start.

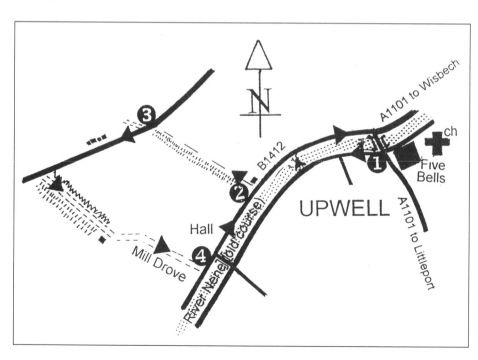

One of the many attractive houses to be found in the village.

PLACES of INTEREST

Wisbech is only 5 miles away and is a very pleasant town to explore. The river Nene flows through the centre of Wisbech on its way to the Wash. Facing the river on each side are many fine old Georgian houses, on both the North Brink and the South Brink. On the North Brink is **Peckover House**, now owned by the National Trust. It was built in 1722. The panelled rooms, fine carvings and plasterwork and the late 18th-century furniture are a delight to see. So are the two acres of gardens. Telephone 01945 583463.

On the South Brink is the birthplace of Octavia Hill, co-founder member of the National Trust, a philanthropist and a tireless worker in Housing Reform. The **Octavia Hill Birthplace Museum** is open to the public on Wednesday, Saturday and Sunday afternoons from March to October. Telephone 01945 476358.

LITTLE THETFORD

Length: 4½ miles (or 2½ miles)

Getting there: Turn off the A10, Cambridge to Ely road, at a minor cross road about 2 miles from Ely. Go in an easterly direction and you will be at the village centre in about ¼ mile.

Parking: Choose a part of the village street which is somewhat wider than the rest, taking care not to obstruct village comings and goings.

Map: OS Landranger – Cambridge etc 154 (GR 532763).

Little Thetford is a delightful small village comprising, in the main, houses fronting a single ¾ mile long cul-de-sac leading from the A10 to a railway crossing. The road continues for a further ¼ mile as a little used track out to the bank of the river Great Ouse. At the centre of the village is a small attractive green. Nearby is the church, and almost opposite is a two storey building, a circular cottage with a steep conical thatched roof. It is easy to assume that its circular wall was the base of a former windmill but this is not the case, it was always a dwelling.

From Little Thetford, this interesting walk starts alongside Grunty Fen Catch-

❷ Pass a cart bridge over the watercourse and keep on following the stream. In about 100 yards, enter a broad grassy track with, on the left beyond the stream, a wood and on the right a ditch bordering a band of mature trees. Cross a stile beside a gate and go straight on.

Keep beside the stream which bends round to the right and, after passing on the left what looks like an assault course beyond the stream, reach the railway. Cross the stiles, carefully cross the line and walk straight on to the river Great Ouse.

❸ Turn right and follow the river upstream. Throughout the walk, but particularly here, there are good views of Ely Cathedral. The route is along a broad riverside flood protection bank with, on the right, parallel to the river a small drainage ditch. On your way you will find a few stiles to cross.

❹ About ¾ mile further on, reach a brick pumping station on the right. The fields on either side of the river tend to be below the river level and pumping stations are very common in this area.

❺ Continue beside the river for 200 yards

water, one of the many drainage ditches which criss-cross this area, and in about a mile you reach the bank of the river Great Ouse. The walk then follows the river, along which narrow boats, motor cruisers and sailing craft travel, particularly in summer. In the winter it is a quieter river and time spent watching birds can be rewarding. After passing its confluence with the river Cam, which flows from Cambridge, the walk returns along a farm road, across fields back to the village.

THE WALK

❶ Walk down Main Street from the chapel. Soon you reach Holt Fen. Here at a sign turn left on a broad track and in about 100 yards swing left to follow a ditch, called Thetford Catchwater, on the left. Keep beside the ditch where it makes a sharp right turn and soon after, it is joined by another ditch, the Grunty Fen Catchwater, on the far side to become a wider stream, flanked by mature willows on its left. Continue on a raised bank, about a yard higher than the neighbouring field.

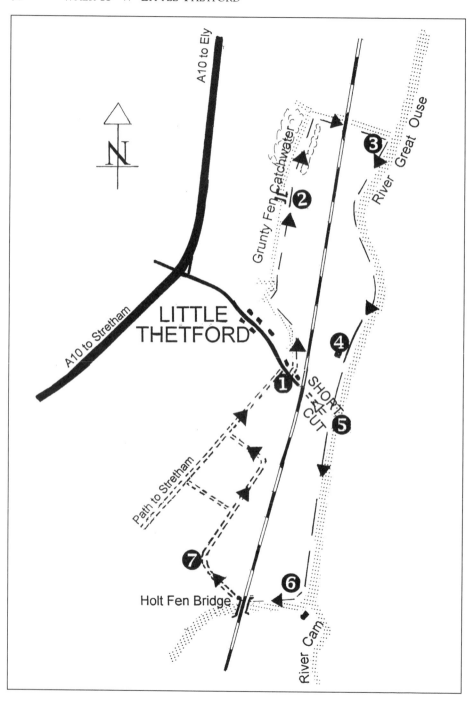

The river Great Ouse, with Ely in the background.

and you reach the end of a road coming from the level crossing at Little Thetford. For those wishing to take a short cut, go right along the road for ¼ mile, back to the start.

Continuing the full walk, just after the road go through a pleasant well tended riverside enclosure. This is a River Authority mooring place for boats which use the river. Keep beside the river.

❻ In about ½ mile pass the confluence of the rivers Cam and Great Ouse. There is a small marina just off the Cam and the Fish and Duck, an old pub which you cannot reach from this side of the Ouse. Keep beside the river. When you get to the rail-

way, go under the bridge, taking care not to hit your head on the girder, and immediately after, go right over a stile down the flood bank and walk away from the river along a grassy farm road edged with trees and a ditch on both sides.

❼ The track makes a turn to the right and in about 200 yards, a waymarked permissive path on the left leads to Stretham (a mile away). Keep straight on along a broad track with trees on the left. The path bends to the left and in 300 yards turn right on to a hard farm road which leads directly back to Little Thetford and the start.

LODE

Length: 4½ miles

Getting there: Lode is about 4 miles north-east of Cambridge. Leave the A14 at the grade-separated intersection on the east side of Cambridge and take the B1102 towards Burwell. In just under 3 miles pass the entrance to Anglesey Abbey and shortly after turn left to the village of Lode.

Parking: There is only roadside parking in the village. The most suitable spot is about halfway along Mill Road, a cul-de-sac on the left beyond the post office. There is a large car park for those visiting Anglesey Abbey, but have regard to closing time, 6 pm.

Map: OS Landranger – Cambridge etc 154 (GR 532627).

The pretty village of Lode is just a stone's throw from Anglesey Abbey (National Trust). The main street is pleasant to wander along, there is an attractive look-ing village hall and a charming group of houses at the bend in the road. Explore Mill Road, a turning by the thatched house with a straw peacock on its ridge. At the end is Lode Mill, beside Quy Water and beyond which lie the gardens of the Abbey.

This figure of eight walk starts at Lode

Mill. The route goes through the village then along a field path to the entrance of Anglesey Abbey, by the car park, where anyone visiting the Abbey, its grounds or café, would probably start. The walk continues back to the mill and thence beside Quy Water for about a mile. The return is along country lanes to Quy Fen and field paths back to Lode.

THE WALK

❶ From Lode Mill walk back along Mill Road and at the T-junction, turn right along the village street. In about 100 yards turn right opposite the post office along a narrow lane past the Baptist chapel.

Turn left at the corner of the burial ground on to an earth path and keep beside a hedge on the left. Pass a house on the right and come out to the head of a cul-de-sac. Go right and soon follow a narrow headland path with a holly hedge on the right, to the field corner.

❷ At this point, the path to the left leads to Anglesey Abbey entrance. This walk continues through the kissing-gate on the right.

Anglesey Abbey.

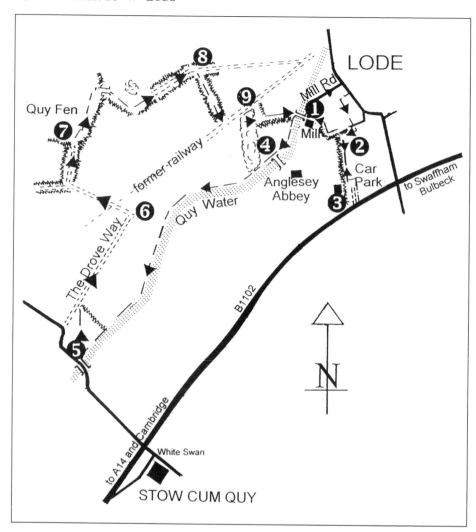

❸ (If starting from the Abbey car park go towards the shop and walk beside the left-hand side of the car park field. Continue to the corner of a field and go through a kissing-gate.)

The gate leads shortly into a meadow. Keep beside a hedge on the left and follow it round the field. After a tennis court on the right go through a gap in a cross-hedge and continue beside an allotment. On reaching a junction of tracks, go left on a narrow path to the white painted mill.

Walk past the front of the mill, cross a wooden footbridge, turn left and climb a small bank to walk beside Quy Water. When a line of mature poplar trees is reached, it is necessary to drop down off the bank to follow a well-used path parallel to the river. As you pass, you can glimpse on the left, beyond the river, Anglesey Abbey gardens.

❹ Pass an ornamental bridge but continue to follow the river bank. About ½ mile from the mill cross a stile and leave the wooded area. Continue on a raised bank beside Quy Water with fields on both sides for another ½ mile.

❺ The riverside path comes to a road with a bridge across the river. However, do not go out to the road but make an almost U-turn to the right and walk away from the river diagonally across the field. At the corner of the field go out and turn right along a lane called The Drove Way.

❻ In under ½ mile the lane makes a sharp left turn and shortly crosses the route of a former railway line. You will see an old thick concrete level crossing gatepost on the left. At a Y-junction of tracks turn right at a waymark into a green lane. Continue to the end of the lane and cross a stile into a meadow called Quy Fen.

❼ After the stile turn right (ignoring the Horningsea Circular Walk sign) and continue through the meadow with a mature hedge on the right. Cross a stile in a timber fence and keep in the same direction as before. Later bear slightly right at a waymark to a stile and cross a long footbridge. From this point the official map shows a cross-field path, but follow a well-used and waymarked headland path with a hedge on the right, round two sides of the field and into a broad green lane.

❽ In about 200 yards, at a waymark turn right along a grassy ride with a ditch, and beyond it a hedge on the left and a hedge on the right. When you reach a cinder track at right angles, turn left along it. The map shows the footpath striking obliquely right across a field, but follow the track.

❾ Pass the end of a wood on the right and immediately after the wood turn right along a narrow path between a hedge and the wood. In 100 yards turn left and follow a well-used headland path leading directly back to Lode Mill.

BALSHAM

Length: 4½ miles

Getting there: From the A11, between Newmarket, and the M11, take the slip road signed Balsham, Fulbourn and Teversham, and turn south. In 3 miles at the edge of Balsham turn left, to reach the centre of the village. Turn left on a narrow road at the end of the green, to the church.

Parking: A limited amount of street parking by the post office, mostly used by shoppers, and a parking area beside the children's playground, close to the recreation ground. Take the road to the church and turn left at the churchyard gate.

Map: OS Landranger – Cambridge etc 154 (GR 586508)

The large village of Balsham lies on the chalklands of south Cambridgeshire and the wide, gently undulating fields are similar to those around Newmarket except that, unlike Newmarket, the area is not given over to rearing horses. Consequently there is little pasture. A mile to the north-west lies the Fleam Dyke, an ancient, probably 7th-century, fortification which, together with the parallel Devils Dyke to the east, defended the East Anglians from invaders in the west. A mile to the south of Balsham is a Roman road, Worstead Street, which ran between Godmanchester and Horseheath.

At the heart of Balsham, between the shops and the lane to the church, is a green on which a many-sided memorial shelter stands. The Icknield Way, a modern version of an ancient trackway, runs through Balsham. A sign on the green records that it is 43 miles to the Peddars Way and 63 miles to the Ridgeway.

If you walk west, away from the small green, passing the large, cream-washed Manor House, you will quickly come to narrow Nine Chimneys Lane. At the end stands the charming old timber-framed house which gives the lane its name. Extremely wealthy Thomas Sutton, who founded Charterhouse school in 1611, was a denizen of Balsham, and had associations with Nine Chimneys House. Charterhouse has ever since been the patron of Balsham church. A former rector, the Revd E J Burrell was a master craftsman in wood; much of his work can be seen in the church, notably the very tall and intricately carved telescopic font cover.

This circular walk takes you south, with extensive views over the countryside, to walk part of the old Roman road, and returns along a pleasant track back to the village.

Charming timber-framed Nine Chimneys House.

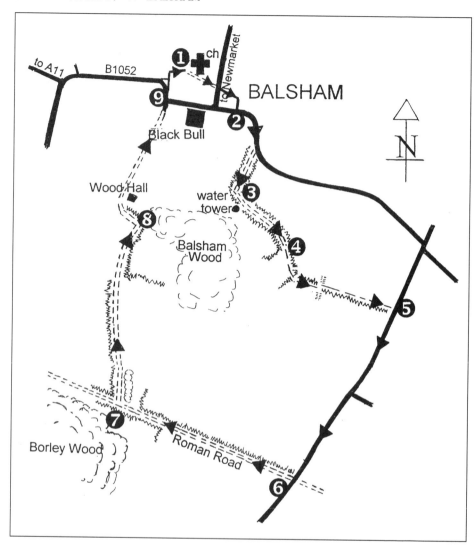

THE WALK

❶ Starting at the churchyard gate, near the children's playground, cross the churchyard. Taking the right fork leave by a gate, into a lane which in 100 yards leads to a road. Cross straight over into Burrell Way and after a bend round to the right come out to a T-junction and go left.

❷ Keep along the road which gradually bends to the right, for about 300 yards. Soon after passing The Brambles on the left, go right on a hard track, signed Public Byway.

❸ The path bends round to the left, passing a concrete water tower, 100 yards away

❼ After ½ mile there is a hedge on both sides of the track, and immediately after passing a few trees in an overgrown hedge on the right, leave the Roman road and turn right along a pleasant lane with a shelter-belt of trees and shrubs on the right and a poor hedge on the left.

❽ Keep on the cart track which in about ½ mile makes a sharp bend to the left. In a further 200 yards follow the lane round a bend to the right. Soon the track becomes surfaced and over to the right you can see the water tower which was passed earlier. Keep straight on, joining Balsham village street at the post office.

❾ From the post office cross the road and walk towards the church, passing the memorial shelter and on the right 'The House on the Green'.

The road goes round past a thatched cottage called 'Long Thatch'. Pass the Church Institute on the left, back to the start.

on the right. Before long the path goes downhill and becomes grassier. The green lane ends at the entrance to a large field with extensive views ahead.

❹ Continue straight on along a narrow headland path, with a hedge on the left. Go through a cross-hedge and continue as before. There is a ditch at the next field corner. Here go 2 yards left, cross a culvert and continue as before but now on a grassy farm track with a hedge on the right.

❺ At the road turn right along the broad verge. In just over ¼ mile, pass a turning on the left to Streetly End and in another ¼ mile, just after going under some electricity wires, a public bridleway crosses the road.

❻ Go right along the former Roman road, a hard flinty track with a hedge on the right.

PRICKWILLOW

Length: 5 ½ miles

Getting there: Prickwillow is about 4 miles east of the City of Ely along the B1382. Cross the river Great Ouse at the edge of Ely. In about 2 miles, in Prickwillow, you reach a substantial bridge over the river Lark. Just by the bridge is the Museum.

Parking: There is a fair amount of on-street parking, and for visitors to the Drainage Engine Museum there is plenty of parking at the rear.

Map: OS Landranger – Ely etc 143 (GR 596825)

The houses of Prickwillow for the most part lie on either side of the main road which, standing on a roddon, is some 2 metres above the level of the land on each side. For a description of how roddons were formed see Walk 11. Before the river Great Ouse was re-routed in a straight line north-east from Ely it used to run in a circuitous way through Prickwillow. Willow trees grew in the wetlands in abundance, and from them were cut the broaches, or prickets, with which thatchers used to fasten the bundles of reeds onto the roof. This is the origin of the village's name.

FOOD and DRINK

A pleasant airy café attached to the Prickwillow Drainage Engine Museum serves tea, coffee, crisps, biscuits and ices. For more substantial meals it is necessary to go beyond the village to Ely, where you could have a meal at the attractive restaurant (telephone: 01353 666360) run by the Cathedral in the very pleasant surroundings of the old almonry. It is situated within the Cathedral boundary wall to the north-east of the Cathedral. All the dishes are home-made.

level of the land dropped, so that in time the minor drains which crisscrossed the land were at a lower level than the rivers into which they were meant to drain.

To overcome this problem of dropping levels, drainage pumps were set up all over the fens to lift the water from the minor drains up into the rivers, so that the surplus water could flow away to the sea, at the Wash. At first the men of the lonely fens saw the land drainage as a threat to their livelihood as wildfowlers and fishermen. They banded together to destroy the drainage system; they were called Fen Tigers. The fascinating story of the drainage of the Fens is told at the Drainage Engine Museum, where the walk, which is through a typical fenland landscape, starts. From Prickwillow Bridge the walk follows the river Lark, mostly

Prickwillow encapsulates the history of the drainage of the fens; it is typical of a community changed from dependency on fishing and wildfowling in a wet landscape to, today, a prosperous farming area. In the 17th century the exceedingly wet land in this part of Cambridgeshire was drained, the peat shrank and consequently the

Goats on the bank of the river Lark.

along the crest of a wide flood protection bank. You pass the Upper Engine House, a former riverside pumping station, with beside it, the attendant's cottage. The walk continues beside the river Great Ouse, where a variety of craft may be seen, towards the City of Ely. The return is along a good hard track with the unromantic name of Second Drove, through rich arable farmland growing a variety of vegetables, sugar beet and corn.

THE WALK

❶ From the road bridge over the river Lark, just by the Drainage Engine Museum, go beside the river along Padnal Bank, with the river on your right. As you approach the railway, move left off the bank and go under the bridge and continue on a narrow farm road beside the river's flood protection bank. Glancing left you will see Ely Cathedral. Shortly pass Bridge Farm.

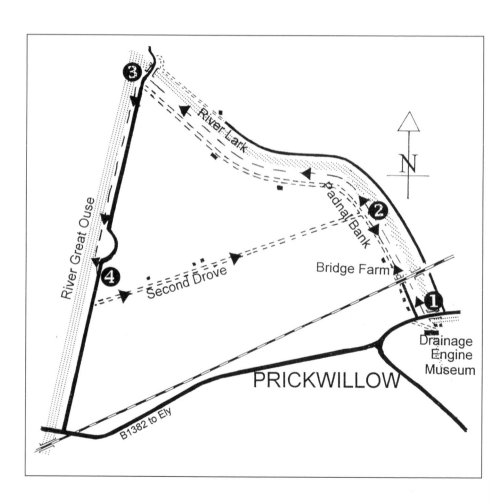

❷ Soon the well-used farm track turns left at a footpath sign. Here go over a stile in the fence on the right and climb the bank, turning left beside the river. In about a mile pass a former pumping station and nearby a house called the Upper Engine House. Eventually cross a stile to a road which crosses the river Lark.

To take a short cut back to Prickwillow, turn right over the bridge and take a gravel farm road on the right to follow the opposite bank of the river.

❸ For the main walk, go left along the road for a few yards and then swing slightly right to walk along the top of the flood protection bank beside the river Great Ouse which flows straight from Ely. Keep on the bank for ¾ mile. The road at the foot of the bank swings to the left to avoid some farm buildings, but keep straight on. Just after the farm, take a shallow ramp alongside the bank which leads down to the road which has swung back to the edge of the bank.

❹ Keep beside the road for 200 yards and then turn left along an unmade farm track called Second Drove. This track runs straight across rich black silty fields growing a variety of crops including vegetables. Eventually the track reaches the river Lark where you were earlier. Turn right and retrace your steps back to the village.

Entrance to the Prickwillow Drainage Engine Museum.

BURROUGH GREEN

Length: 4½ miles

Getting there: From Newmarket take the B1061 towards Haverhill. One mile beyond Dullingham turn sharp left (still on the B1061) and in ½ mile reach Burrough Green.	**Parking:** It is possible to park by the green, on the long side remote from the main road. There is plenty of customer parking behind the Bull public house.	**Map:** OS Landranger – Cambridge etc 154 (GR 637554).

Burrough Green centres on an enormous, well-kept green. At one end is the village pub, the Bull, and the various school buildings which cluster at the end of the green, and at the other end is the cricket square and pavilion. The green is crossed by a road which leads to the church of St

Augustine. The church is unusual in that on both the south and north sides there are three gables just east of the tower.

High on the front of the oldest of the school buildings, behind the willow tree, are two delightful sculptures, featuring in deep relief, one a boy and the other a girl

FOOD and DRINK

The Bull has an interesting menu, which includes vegetarian dishes, and the food is plentiful. Cashew casserole, asparagus quiche, sausage, cod and plaice, with cheesecake, lemon meringue or deep-filled apple tart to follow are available. On Thursdays fresh fish is a speciality.

Around the walls are pictures of cricketers and lots about cricket. The villagers of Burrough Green take their cricket seriously. Telephone: 01638 507480.

in the dress of the 1700s. In 1734 the charity school was founded by the rector, Dr Samuel Knight. A band at the rim of each says: 'Train up a child' and 'Naked and ye clothed me'.

The Icknield Way which runs across south-east England, from Ivinghoe Beacon in Buckinghamshire to Knettishall Heath in Suffolk, crosses the green at Burrough Green. Starting along the Icknield Way, the walk goes to the village of Brinkley, passing within view of Brinkley Hall, and then to Willingham Green where a lane leads down to cross the river Stour, about ½ mile from its source at Weston Green. The Stour flows south-eastwards to a wide estuary at Harwich and for much of its length it forms the boundary between Suffolk and Essex. The walk continues to Carlton Hill and returns, re-crossing the river Stour and passing Park Wood, to Burrough Green.

THE WALK

❶ At the Green, take the minor road almost opposite the Bull, across the Green, and at the far side turn left at an Icknield Way sign along Sheriffs Court.

The delightful sculptures above the door of the old school on the green.

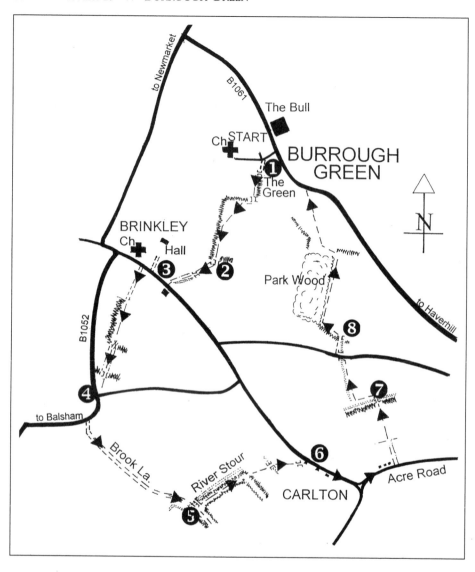

Where the concrete ends turn right over a footbridge, through a kissing-gate and turn left, following a hedge on the left. At the corner of the field go over a stile and a sleeper bridge and turn right for a few yards. Then swing left on a grass path across the corner of the field. Swing half left at the hedge and continue on a broad headland with fine views to the left.

❷ At the field corner keep straight on across a bridge and a stile, and follow a fence on the right through a meadow to a footbridge. This leads into a narrow path and out through a kissing-gate to a road almost opposite Brinkley Memorial Hall.

❸ Turn right along the road and about 100 yards beyond Hall Lane on the right, and close to Brinkley church, turn left along Coles Lane beside a green on the left. Soon the lane becomes a fine grassy headland with a hedge on the right. At the corner of the field go over a stile and straight on between paddocks. Go through a kissing-gate to cross a pasture to a narrow, close-boarded kissing-gate to a T-junction at Willingham Green Lane.

❹ Go along the B1052 towards Linton for about 200 yards and turn left on a grassy track called Brook Lane. Gradually the lane descends into a shallow valley and in nearly ½ mile, fords the tiny river Stour.

❺ Cross the bridge beside the ford and immediately after, turn left along a narrower green lane following the river on the left. In about ¼ mile, and soon after passing a footbridge on the left, the lane makes a bend to the right. A few yards beyond the bend, turn left at a waymark and bearing a little to the right, take a cross-field path. Cross a sleeper bridge with a handrail and continue in the same direction. On the far side of the field enter a narrow grass path through a wild garden, crossing a bridge and a stile, out to a road at Carlton Hill.

❻ Turn right along the road and in 300 yards turn left along Acre Road. Descend the slight hill and just after Acre Cottage on the left, and before a house on the

---

---

right, turn left over a stile into a narrow footpath through the edge of a garden. Cross another stile into a pasture and keep beside the fence on the right. Cross a stile beside a pair of white gates and enter a large field. Follow the waymark straight ahead. When you get further into the field make for a stile under some trees in the valley bottom.

❼ Cross the river Stour and turn left on a headland. At the field corner turn right and keep beside a small ditch on the left. At the road go left over a bridge and immediately turn right to follow the ditch on the right.

❽ Cross a wide ditch and turn left on a headland path towards Park Wood. At the corner turn right, climbing slightly beside the wood. At the top corner of Park Wood keep straight on for a few yards to the end of a hedge and turn left beside the cultivation, going towards a hedge about 200 yards away. At or near the hedge turn half right on a reinstated path going towards the white painted Wyck Farm. At the road go left to the Green and the start.

SNAILWELL

Length: 5 miles

Getting there: Snailwell is a mile from the A14 road, just north of Newmarket. Leave the A14 Bury to Cambridge road at the A142 interchange and go towards Ely. About 300 yards from the interchange, turn right for Snailwell, and in 1 mile swing left at a wide grassy triangle to the village centre.

Parking: There is no village car park. The George and Dragon pub has a customer car park.

Otherwise, parking in Church Lane towards the church gate would seem reasonable.

Map: OS Landranger – Cambridge etc 154 (GR642677).

Snailwell, a small village at the edge of Newmarket, depends greatly on horse-racing. Just to the south of the village are the well appointed buildings of Snailwell Stud alongside which, facing the Newmarket road, is a fine, life-size, bronze statue of a black horse, by John Skeaping. Still within the parish, but close to Newmarket, is the British Horseracing School.

Equine influence is not quite so apparent in the village centre where, shaded by mature trees, a number of attractive houses

❶ From Church Lane walk northwards along the road towards Fordham, passing the George and Dragon public house on the left.

❷ One hundred yards beyond the last house, turn right along a broad grassy green lane. In 200 yards the track bends slightly left and crosses a large open field. After going through a narrow shelter belt of trees and bushes keep on beside a crop division for ½ mile to reach a farm track at right angles.

❸ Turn left along this well used track towards a wood 200 yards away. Cross the stile beside a white gate to enter the Chippenham Fen National Nature Reserve on a broad grassy way. Keep straight on through the reserve, crossing a cart bridge over a small stream, immediately followed by a stile beside a gate. Keep on the track.

FOOD and DRINK

The food at the George and Dragon is good, quite a lot of it being home-made. The pub specializes in fish dishes. On the menu are Barbary duck breast, fisherman's platter, salmon shantie, salmon and halibut Wellington and Provençal nut Wellington. Parents should be aware that the river is just at the bottom of the garden. Telephone: 01638 577241.

---

and cottages, some old, some modern, are grouped together in the vicinity of the church and the public house nearby. The pond at the west end of the church is the source of the river Snail, later to become the Soham Lode, a tributary of the river Cam.

At the north end of the main street is a delightful terrace of three flint-faced cottages, reminding us that the underlying strata in this part of Cambridge is chalk, and flint was a common building material in times past. St Peter's church tower is one of only two round church towers in Cambridgeshire. Part of the church dates from 1070. Close to Church Lane is a house, with a clock atop the roof, which was the village school.

This walk is across field paths to the Chippenham National Nature Reserve, a shallow peat-filled valley where reeds and sedges flourish, and where among water-loving trees and scrub, a rich variety of plant and insect life abounds. After following the public footpath through the reserve, the walk reaches Chippenham village, returning to Snailwell on quiet field paths.

PLACES of INTEREST

The National Horseracing Museum is in Newmarket High Street, next to the Jockey Club. It is open from the end of March to the beginning of December, Tuesday through to Saturday, plus Monday in July and August, from 10 am till 5 pm, also Sunday from 12 noon till 4 pm. Telephone: 01638 667333.

At the **National Stud**, at the edge of Newmarket, guided tours, which must be booked, take place from the end of March to the beginning of October on weekdays at 11.15 am and 2.30 pm, at 11.15 am on Saturday and at 2.30 pm on Sunday. Telephone: 01638 663464.

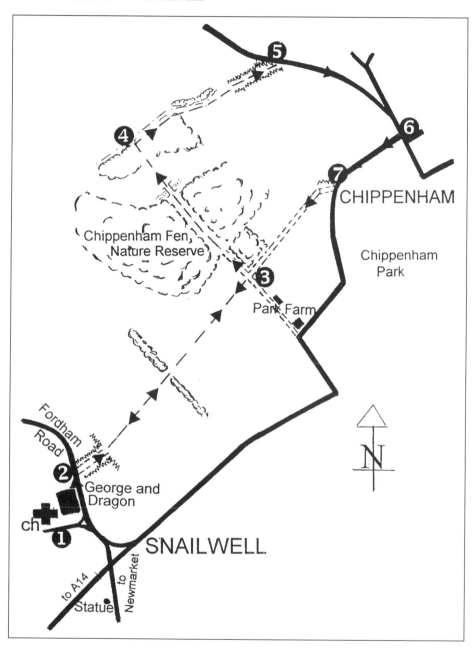

The George & Dragon public house.

❹ Eventually, in about ½ mile from the entrance to the Fen, reach a fence at right angles, turn right and follow, on the left, the fence and later having crossed a stile, a windbreak of pines. Leave the reserve by a stile and follow a green lane which leads out to a road.

❺ Turn right along the B1085 into Chippenham.

❻ In the village, at a T-junction by the village well, turn right opposite the Tharp Arms into Palace Lane.

❼ In ¼ mile, where the road swings left, go half-right on a grassy headland with a hedge on the right. When the hedge ends continue on across a large field. As you approach the far side of the field there is a plantation of conifers on the right. At the field boundary meet the farm road at right angles which you reached earlier before turning towards the Nature Reserve. Go straight on, retracing your steps to Snailwell along the path you used earlier.